AF396407

VISUAL CULTURES AS
OBJECTS AND AFFECTS

JORELLA ANDREWS
SIMON O'SULLIVAN

Sternberg Press

JORELLA ANDREWS

Visual culture emerged in the mid-1990s as a new—or, rather, a newly articulated—field of inquiry that attempted to reintegrate a wide range of visual, artistic, philosophical, cultural, and political concerns. Cross-disciplinary in nature, it has become a site of encounter for divergent perspectives, including competing attitudes toward the ethical status and ideological functioning of the visual itself. Emerging from interactions between scholars, artists, curators, and activists, visual culture has also encouraged multilayered, often hybrid, modes of investigation. These have done much to extend, even reposition, intellectual research beyond the traditional parameters of the university.

Given visual culture's highly differentiated character, this series of short coauthored books is not intended to be a comprehensive collection of representative texts. Indeed, its starting point—in the Visual Cultures department at Goldsmiths—was a discussion about our own diverse investments in this still-evolving field. Each publication, therefore, invites a multifaceted investigation of a single, pertinent topic. In each case, two colleagues with shared interests—and differing points of view—examine their chosen subject in a particularized and probing manner. The format is always the same: two essays and a conversation. But within this scheme, contents unfold in their own way with respect to their positions, polemics, and poetics. In some instances, it's been appropriate to combine newly commissioned work with essays that were written some time ago, or with material that has existed, until now, in lecture form only. The conversations, staged for the purpose of these volumes, provide fruitful context and offer a first layer of reflection and response in what are emphatically open and ongoing debates.

SIMON O'SULLIVAN

Art is thus confused with a cultural object and may give rise to any of the discourses to which anthropological data in general lend themselves. One could do a history, sociology, or political economy of it, to mention just those few. One can easily show that its destination, anthropologically speaking, undergoes considerable modification depending on whether the artwork "belongs" to a culture that is tribal, imperial, republican, monarchical, theocratic, mercantile, autocratic, capitalist, and so on, and that it is a determining feature of the contemporary work that it is obviously destined for the museum (collection, conservation, exhibition) and for the museum audience. This approach is implied in any "theory" of art, for the theory is made only of objects, in order to determine them. But the work is not merely a cultural object, although it is that too. It harbours within it an excess, a rapture, a potential of associations that overflows all the determinations of its "reception" and "production."
Jean-François Lyotard, "Critical Reflections"

How could it happen that in thinking about art, in reading the art object, we missed what art does best? In fact, we missed that which defines art: the aesthetic—because art is not an object among others, at least not an object of knowledge (or not only an object of knowledge). Rather, art does something else. Indeed, art is precisely antithetical to knowledge; it works against what Jean-François Lyotard once called the "fantasies of realism."[1] Which is to say that art might well be a part of the world (after all it is a made thing), but at the same time it is apart from the world. And this apartness, however it is theorized, is what constitutes art's importance.

In this essay I want to think a little about this apartness; this "excess" or "rapture" that, as Lyotard remarks above, constitutes art's effectivity over and above its existence as a cultural object. I want to claim that this excess need not be theorized as transcendent; we can think the aesthetic power of art in an immanent sense, through recourse to the notion of *affect.*

Before moving on, however, a backward glance: What happened? What caused this aesthetic blindness? In the discipline of art history there were, are, (at least) two factors in play. First, Marxism (or "The Social History of Art")—that is, the propensity to explain art historically, through recourse to its moment of production. Second, deconstruction (or "The New Art History")—the propensity to stymie (historical) interpretations while still inhabiting their general explanatory framework. Marxism and deconstruction: understanding art as representation, and then understanding art as being implicated in the crisis in representation; appealing to origins as final explanation, and then putting the notion of origin under erasure. First aesthetics fell foul of Marxism: A disinterested beauty? A transcendent aesthetic? Ideological![2] Then it fell foul of deconstruction; the apparatus of capture that is deconstruction, Jacques Derrida neatly reconfiguring the discourse of aesthetics as a discourse of/on representation. Aesthetics is deconstructed, and art becomes a broken promise.[3] Both Marxism and deconstruction were, and still are, powerful critiques. However, deconstruction especially is negative critique *par excellence*; indeed, it is implicitly a critique of Marxism—and Karl Marx and Derrida will always be troublesome bedfellows, at least in this sense.

Deconstructive reading is not in and of itself a bad thing. Indeed, it might be strategically important to employ deconstruction precisely to counteract the effects of, to disable, a certain kind of aesthetic discourse: deconstruction as a kind of expanded ideological critique. However, after the deconstructive reading, the art object remains. Life goes on. Art, whether we will it or not, continues producing affects. What is the "nature" of affects, and can they be deconstructed? Affects can be described as extra-discursive and extra-textual.[4] Affects are moments of intensity, a reaction in/on the body at the level of matter.[5] We might even say that affects are immanent to matter—they are certainly immanent to experience. (Following Baruch Spinoza, we might define affect as the effect another body, an art object, for example, has upon my own body and my body's *duration*.)[6] As such, affects are not to do with knowledge or meaning; indeed, they occur on a different register—an asignifying register.[7] In fact, this is what differentiates art from language—although language, too, can and does have an affective register (indeed, signification itself might be understood as a complex affective function; meaning would thus be the effect of affects).

Of course, from a certain perspective, affects are only meaningful within language. Indeed, affects can be "understood," can be *figured*, as always already a representation of what we might call the Ur- or originary affect—the latter positioned as an unreachable (and unsayable) origin. Again, so much for deconstruction. And yet affects are also, and primarily, affective. There is no denying or deferring affects. They are what make up life—and art.[8] For there is a sense in which art itself is made up of affects: affects frozen in time and space. Affects are (to use Deleuzo-Guattarian terms, and to move the register away from deconstruction and away from representation) the *molecular* "beneath" the *molar*—the molecular understood here as life's, and art's, intensive quality, as the stuff that goes on beneath, beyond, even parallel to, signification.[9]

But what can one say about affects? Indeed, what needs to be said about them? Certainly, in a space such as art history where deconstructive—let alone semiotic—approaches to art are becoming, indeed have become, hegemonic, the existence of affects, and their central role in art, needs asserting. For this is what art is: a bundle of affects, or, as Gilles Deleuze and Félix Guattari would say, a *bloc of sensations*, waiting to be reactivated by a spectator or participant.[10] Indeed, you cannot read affects, you can only experience them. Which brings us to the crux of the matter: experience. Paul de Man, as a more or less typical spokesperson for that melancholy science that is deconstruction, writes, "It is a temporal experience of human mutability, historical in the deepest sense of the term in that it implies the necessary experience of any present as a *passing* experience, that makes the past irrevocable and unforgettable, because it is inseparable from any present or future."[11]

As with Derrida, so with de Man: present experience—the moment, the event—is inaccessible to consciousness. All we ever have is its trace; we experience "passing" moments. If affects "are" precisely present experience, it could be said, following de Man et al., that all we ever have is a kind of echo, the representation of affect. Now this is a clever and beguiling story, giving affects a logocentric spin. But, I wonder, are affects really of this type? Is affect transcendent in this sense? Beyond experience? Or, rather, is it not the case, as I have already suggested, that affects are *immanent* to experience,[12] and that all this writing about affect is really just that: writing—writing that produces an effect of representation. (Parodying Derrida a little, we might say that by asking the question "What is an affect?" we are already presupposing that there is an answer—an answer which must be given in language. We have, in fact, placed affect in a conceptual opposition that always and everywhere promises, and then frustrates, meaning.)

So much for writing—and for art as a kind of writing. In fact, an affect is something else entirely: precisely an event or happening. Indeed, this is what defines affect. It is not that de Man (or Derrida for that matter) is wrong: as subjects we certainly can be positioned, and position ourselves, in de Man's temporal predicament (a name for which is representation). This has often been the way in the West—in modernism and in postmodernism. Indeed, we might say, in the wake of Michael Fried and his detractors, that this oscillation between aesthetics and its deconstruction has animated the discourse of art history up to today.[13] But this deconstructive mechanism, this way of thinking art (and ourselves), inevitably closes down the possibility of accessing the event that is art. Indeed, within this mechanism art is either positioned as transcendent or, with deconstruction, is always already positioned and predetermined by the discourse that surrounds it—the event as always already captured by representation. Art, here, becomes a broken promise, a fallen angel.

But is this the end of the story? Might there, in fact, be a way of rescuing art from this predicament, this double bind, without necessarily returning to a traditional transcendent aesthetic? Indeed, how might we think art as event? This is a slippery area—and much recent philosophy has been written on how to think the event.[14] It is almost a question of faith: either you side with deconstruction (the event as always already constituted, determined by the scene of the event), or you get a little more religious (the event as something genuinely unexpected). Importantly, this need not involve a transcendent aesthetic—no return to Clement Greenberg, no return to Immanuel Kant.

In fact, there may be a way of reconfiguring the event as *immanent* to this world, as not arriving from any kind of transcendent plane (and as not transporting us there) but as emerging from the realm of the virtual. In the realm of the virtual, art—artwork—is no longer an object as such, or not only an object, but rather a space, a *zone*[15]—what Alain Badiou might call an "event site"—"a point of exile where it is possible that something, finally, might happen."[16] At any rate, art is a place where one might encounter affect. Such an accessing of the event might involve what Henri Bergson calls *attention*: a suspension of normal motor activity that in itself allows other "planes" of reality to be perceivable; an opening up to the world beyond utilitarian interests.[17] Following Bergson, we might say that, as beings in the world, we are caught on a certain spatiotemporal register: we see only what we have already seen; we see only what we are interested in. At stake with art, then, might be an altering, a switching, of this register. New (prosthetic) technologies can achieve this switching of temporal registers: time-lapse photography producing firework flowers and flows of traffic; slow-motion film revealing intricate movements that otherwise are a blur. They can achieve a switching of spatial registers too: microscopes and telescopes showing us the molecular and the super-molar. At this point, we might say, new media coincide with art: indeed, new media take on an *aesthetic* function, a *deterritorializing* function. But, we need not turn to new technologies. The realm of affects is all around us, and there are as many different strategies for accessing it as there are subjects. For Deleuze and Guattari, these two sorcerers, it is a question of making yourself a body without organs, understood in this context as a strategy for accessing that which is normally "outside" yourself: your "experimental milieu" that everywhere accompanies your sense of self.[18] This is, according to them, a pragmatic project: you do not just read about the body without organs—you make yourself one.

Georges Bataille talks about such a pragmatic project in his book *Prehistoric Painting*.[19] For Bataille, such a project, such a ritual as the prehistoric cave paintings at Lascaux, can be understood as the creation of a sacred space. Indeed art, for Bataille, is precisely a mechanism for accessing a kind of immanent *beyond* to everyday experience; art operates as a kind of play that takes the participant out of mundane consciousness (hence Bataille's understanding of the Lascaux cave paintings as performative). This might involve a representational function (after all, we can recognize the animals at Lascaux), but representation is not these paintings' sole purpose, and we miss something essential about them if we attend merely to their history—that is, if we simply read them. Lyotard is perhaps most attuned to this experimental and rupturing quality of art. Lyotard calls for a practice of patience, of listening—a kind of meditative state that allows for, produces an opening for, an experience of the event understood as affect. In *Peregrinations*, Lyotard writes:

> [One must] become open to the "It happens that" rather than the "What happens" [… and this] requires at the very least a high degree of refinement in the perception of small differences. [...] In order to take on this attitude you have to impoverish your mind, clean it out as much as possible, so that you make it incapable of anticipating the meaning, the "What" of the "It happens..." The secret of such ascesis

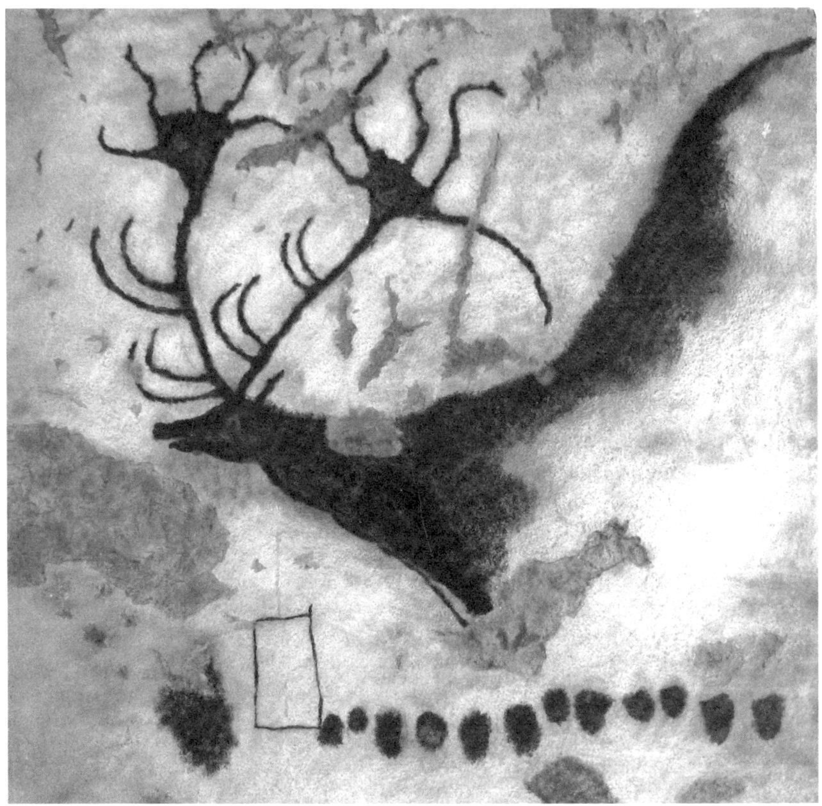

MEGALOCEROS, IN THE AXIAL GALLERY, LASCAUX. PUBLIC DOMAIN (WIKIMEDIA COMMONS).

lies in the power to be able to endure occurrences as "directly" as possible without the mediation of a "pre-text." Thus to encounter the event is like bordering on nothingness.[20]

And so this event, this affect (as Bataille also teaches us), is not really about self-consciousness—the representation of experience to oneself, the self as constituted through representation—at all. In fact, we might say that affect is a more brutal, apersonal thing: it is that which connects us to the world; it is the matter in us responding and resonating with the matter around us. Affect is, in this sense, transhuman. Indeed, with affect, what we have is a kind of transhuman *aesthetic*. De Man might *figure* art as a shield from mortality, a reassuring mirror to a fearful subject (and then, of course, demonstrate that the shield is always already broken), but art is something much more dangerous: a portal, an access point to another world—a world of impermanence and interpenetration, a molecular world of becoming (our world, perhaps, but experienced differently). According to Deleuze and Guattari, this is, ultimately, what makes painting *abstract*: the "summoning" and making visible of forces.[21]

This world of affects, this universe of forces, is our own world seen without the spectacles of subjectivity. But how to remove these spectacles, which are not really spectacles at all but the very condition of our subjectivity? How, indeed, to sidestep our selves? In fact, we do it all the time—we are involved in molecular processes that go on beyond our subjectivity. Indeed we are these processes.[22] We are—in addition to being subjects (bound by *strata*)—bundles of events, bundles of affects, and in a constant process of destratification.[23] At stake here, then, are practices and strategies that reveal this "other side" to ourselves; practices that imaginatively and pragmatically switch the register. After all, why not try something new? As Deleuze remarks in an interview: "What we're interested in, you see, are modes of individuation beyond those of things, persons or subjects: the individuation, say, of a time of day, of a region, a climate, a river or a wind, of an event. And maybe it's a mistake to believe in the existence of things, persons, or subjects."[24]

This is art's function: to switch our intensive register, to reconnect us with the world. Art opens us up to the nonhuman universe that we are part of. Art might well have a representational function—after all, art objects, like everything else, can be read. But art also operates as a fissure in representation. And we, as spectators, as representational creatures, are involved in a dance with art, a dance in which—through careful maneuvers—the molecular is opened up, the aesthetic is activated, and art enacts its chief modus operandi: it transforms, if only for a moment, our sense of our "selves," and our notion of our world.

This is, of course, to claim quite an importance for art. Certainly, it is to move far away from those postmodernists who assert that it is time for art to be included within the "broader picture of representational practices in contemporary society."[25] Indeed, it is to claim a kind of autonomy for art. But, although it may appear so, this autonomy is not the same as, for example, Theodor W. Adorno's. It is, in fact, a reconfiguration of aesthetics away from Adorno and the whole Kantian heritage. In *Aesthetic Theory*, Adorno writes: "Art's utopia, the counter-factual yet-to-come is draped in Black, it goes on being a recollection of the possible with a critical edge against the real. [...] It is the possible, as promised by its impossibility. Art is the promise of happiness, a promise that is constantly being broken."[26]

For Adorno, art operates as a utopian blink: it presents the possible through its difference to the existent. Indeed, art, for Adorno, is not really of this world at all—it prefigures and promises a world yet-to-come. Art, if you like, operates within Walter Benjamin's *messianic time*. And yet art is inevitably doomed to frustration: the promise (of reconciliation) is constantly being broken. Art necessarily operates within this melancholy field. It is worth noting that philosophy, for Adorno, operates on the same register: "The only philosophy which can be reasonably practised in the face of despair is the attempt to contemplate all things as they would present themselves from the standpoint of redemption."[27] In a sense, then, Adorno has abandoned the existent—his is a forsaken world, and this is what gives his work its melancholy tenor.

However, we might want to turn from Adorno to Deleuze, and to a more affirmative notion of the aesthetic impulse. Here, instead of the existent and the possible as ontological categories and as coordinates for art, we can utilize Deleuze's categories of the actual and the virtual. In *Difference and Repetition*, Deleuze outlines this shift, and the difference between the two sets of categories, as follows: "The only danger in all this is that the virtual could be confused with the possible. The possible is opposed to the real; the process undergone by the possible is therefore a 'realisation.' By contrast, the virtual is not opposed to the real; it possesses a full reality by itself. The process it undergoes is actualisation. It would be wrong to see only a verbal dispute here: it is a question of existence itself."[28] At stake in art is not a utopian (and correlatively negative) aesthetic, but an affirmative actualization of the virtual—the latter being a genuinely creative act (as opposed to the realization of the possible, which ultimately and necessarily resembles the real).[29] The virtual, here, can be understood as the realm of affects. Art actualizes these invisible universes;[30] or at least it opens up a portal onto these other, virtual worlds (we might say that art is situated on the borderline between the actual and the virtual).[31] This gives art an ethical imperative, because it involves a kind of moving beyond the already familiar (the human), precisely a kind of self-overcoming.

For Guattari, this new ethico-aesthetic paradigm pertains not just to art but to subjectivity as well (in fact, notions of subject and object become blurred here). Guattari argues that by allowing individuals access to "new materials of expression," "new complexes of subjectivation" become possible; new "incorporeal universes of reference" are opened up that allow for what he calls a process of resingularization—a process of reordering ourselves and our relation to the world.[32] In such a pragmatic, and aesthetic, reconfiguration "one creates new modalities of subjectivity in the same way an artist creates new forms from a palette."[33] (La Borde clinic, where he worked, was understood by Guattari as a *machinic assemblage*, and as precisely a site of resingularization.) But, in fact, people resingularize themselves every day: academics plant allotments, manual laborers visit the theater. Different activities take on aesthetic, deterritorializing functions.

This is to take art away from the Frankfurt School register. For Adorno, art's importance lay, at least in one sense, in its uselessness, its irreducibility to conceptual thought. Art did not partake in, and accordingly provided a critique of, instrumental reason and its accompaniment, the world commodity system. With Deleuze and Guattari and their allies, we have a different mapping of the world, and of philosophy's and art's role within it. Philosophy is no longer to be understood as a utopian pursuit,[34] but is rather to do with pragmatics: active concept creation in order to solve problems, to get something done. Likewise with art: art is not useless; it performs very specific roles.[35] These roles or *functions* differ, depending on the kind of art, and the milieu in which a work of art exists—indeed, Conceptual art might have more in common with what Deleuze and Guattari call philosophy (and the posing of problems). Installation art, on the other hand, might be a paradigmatic case of art as access point to other worlds. Julia Kristeva arrives at precisely this conclusion (here she is writing about contemporary installations at the 45th Venice Biennale in 1993):

> In an installation it is the *body* in its entirety which is asked to participate through its sensations, through *vision* obviously, but also *hearing, touch,* on occasions *smell.* As if these artists, in the place of an "object" sought to place us in a space at the limits of the sacred, and asked us not to contemplate images but to communicate with beings. I had the impression that [the artists] were communicating this: that the ultimate aim of art is perhaps what was formerly celebrated under the term of *incarnation.* I mean by that a wish to make us feel, through the abstractions, the forms, the colours, the volumes, the sensations, a *real experience.*[36]

For Kristeva, art (in this case, installation art) is a bloc of sensations made up of abstractions, forms, colors, and volumes. This art is also a sacred space whose aim it is to give us a real (in this case, multisensory) experience. Kristeva talks about these installations not in terms of representation, but in terms of their function—a function of incarnation. For Kristeva, this aesthetic function is the "ultimate aim of art."

In a sense, this is to move to a *post-medium* notion of art practice in that it is not so important what the specifics of a medium might be (no Greenbergian truth to materials, no more asking "what is art?," "what is painting?," and, thus, no more deconstructions); rather, what becomes important is what a particular art object can do. In relation to aesthetics and affects, this function might be summed up as the making visible of the invisible, the making perceptible of the imperceptible or, as Deleuze and Guattari would say, the harnessing of forces.[37] Another way of saying this is that art is a deterritorialization, a creative deterritorialization into the realm of affects.

Art, then, might be understood as the name for a function: a magical, an aesthetic function of *transformation*. Art is less involved in making sense of the world, and more involved in exploring the possibilities of being—of becoming—in the world; less involved in knowledge, and more involved in experience, in pushing forward the boundaries of what can be experienced;[38] finally, less involved in shielding us from death, but precisely involved in actualizing the possibilities of life. Paradoxically, the notion of an "aesthetic function" might well return us to a productive utilization of the term "visual culture." But this will be a return marked by its passage through aesthetics, through Adorno and Deleuze especially. In a sense, this passage—this championing of art as an autonomous, aesthetic practice—was only the first moment; the second moment being a detachment of the aesthetic from its apparent location within, and transcendent attachment to, certain objects (the canonical objects of art history). This *immanent* aesthetic, as function, can now be thought in relation to a variety of objects and practices. So, yes, perhaps we can speak of a kind of visual culture after all, not through the notion of a general semiotics, but rather through the notion of a general aesthetics.

How might this affect the practice of art history? A certain kind of art history might disappear: that which attends only to art's signifying character, that which understands art, positions art*work* as representation. These latter functions might, however, be placed alongside art's asignifying functions: art's affective and intensive qualities; the molecular beneath, within, the molar. In this place art becomes a more complex, and a more interesting, object. And the business of art history changes from a hermeneutic to a heuristic activity: art history as a kind of parallel to the work that art is already doing, rather than as an attempt to fix and interpret art—art history, perhaps, as precisely a kind of *creative* writing. So I end this essay, this skirmish against representation, with the outline of a new project: the thinking of specific artworks, the writing on specific artworks, the exploration of art's creative, aesthetic, and ethical function.[39] This will involve attending to the specificity of an artwork, and the specificity of the milieu in which the art object operates. This is by no means a retreat from art history, but a reconfiguration of its practice—a reconfiguration that might well involve, as one of its strategies, a return to those writers who have always seen the aesthetic as the function of art, and to those writers who, though they might not be art historians, are nevertheless attuned to the aesthetics of affect.

This text was originally published in *Angelaki: Journal of the Theoretical Humanities* 6, no. 3 (2001): 125–35.

1   Jean-François Lyotard, *The Postmodern Condition: A Report on Knowledge*, trans. Geoff Bennington and Brian Massumi (Manchester: Manchester University Press, 1984), 93.

2   Indeed, there is a "tradition" of positioning critical art history as a form of ideological critique, and specifically as a critique of aesthetics. See, for example, Kurt W. Forster's polemical essay, "Critical History of Art, or a Transfiguration of Values?," *New Literary History* 3, no. 3 (Spring 1972): 459–70.

3   Derrida performs precisely this deconstruction of aesthetics in Jacques Derrida, "The Parergon," in *The Truth in Painting*, trans. Geoff Bennington and Ian McCleod (Chicago: University of Chicago Press, 1987), 37–82.

4   They can be described as extra-discursive in the sense that they are "outside" discourse understood as structure (they are precisely what is irreducible to structure). They can be described as extra-textual in the sense that they do not produce—or do not produce only—knowledge. Affects might, however, be understood as textual in that they are felt as differences in intensity.

5   For Brian Massumi, in "The Autonomy of Affect," affects are likewise understood as moments of intensity. The latter might resonate with linguistic expression but are, strictly speaking, of a different and prior order. For Massumi, as for myself, "approaches to the image in its relation to language are incomplete if they operate only on the semantic or semiotic level, however that level is defined (linguistically, logically, narratologically, ideologically, or all of these combinations, as a Symbolic). What they lose, precisely, is the event—in favour of structure." Brian Massumi, "The Autonomy of Affect," in *Deleuze: A Critical Reader*, ed. Paul Patton (Oxford: Blackwell, 1989), 220.

Massumi identifies the realm of affect as one of increasing importance within "media, literary and art theory," but points out the problem that there is "no cultural-theoretical vocabulary specific to affect." Indeed, our "entire vocabulary has derived from theories of signification that are still wedded to structure" (ibid., 221). From one perspective, Massumi is right: there is no vocabulary of affect. But it is not so simple as inventing one. To invent a language for/of affect is to bring the latter into representation—and hence to invite deconstruction. In a sense, there is no way out of this predicament—other than to acknowledge it as a problem, and move beyond it (which is what this essay attempts to do).

6   See Deleuze's "Spinoza and the Three Ethics," where "affect" is defined as the effect affections have on the body's duration, the "passages, becomings, rises and falls, continuous variations of power (*puissance*) that pass from one state to another. We will call them affects, strictly speaking, and no longer affections. They are signs of increase and decrease, signs that are vectorial (of the joy–sadness type) and no longer scalar like the affections, sensations or perceptions." Gilles Deleuze, "Spinoza and the Three Ethics," in *Essays Critical and Clinical*, trans. Dan W. Smith and Michael A. Greco (London: Verso, 1998), 139.

7   As Guattari observes in an interview: "The same semiotic material can be functioning in different registers. A material can be both caught in paradigmatic chains of production, chains of signification [...] but at the same time can function in an asignifying register. [...] So what determines the difference? In one case, a signifier functions in what one might call a logic of discursive aggregates, i.e. a logic of representation. In the other case, it functions in something that isn't entirely a logic, what I've called an existential machinic, a logic of bodies without organs, a machinic of bodies without organs." Félix Guattari, "Pragmatic/Machinic: Discussion with Félix Guattari," March 19, 1985, http://topologicalmedialab.net/xinwei/classes/readings/Guattari/Pragmatic-Machinic_chat.html.

8   For Guattari, affects can be understood as establishing a kind of center or "self-affirmation" that occurs parallel to the discursive (what Guattari terms "linear") elements of subjectivity. For Guattari, this affective element is present in Sigmund Freud's theory of the drives, but has been overlooked by "the structuralists" (Guattari has Lacan in mind). See Félix Guattari, "On Machines," trans. Vivian Constantinopoulos,

in *Complexity: Architecture/Art/Philosophy*, ed. Andrew E. Benjamin (London: Academy, 1989), 8–12. Guattari writes:

> I consider that limiting ourselves to this coordinate [linearity] is precisely to lose the element of the machinic centre, of subjective autopoiesis and self-affirmation. Whether located at the level of the complete individual or partial subjectivity, or even at the level of social subjectivity, this element undergoes a *pathic* relationship by means of the affect. What is it, then, that makes us state phenomenologically that something is living? It is precisely this relation of affect. This is not a description, nor a kind of propositional analysis resulting from a sense of hypotheses and deductions—i.e., it is a living being, therefore it is a machine; rather an immediate, pathic and non-discursive apprehension occurs of the machine's ontological autocomposition relationship. (Ibid., 10.)

In "On Machines" Guattari develops the notion of a non-discursive, affective foyer, which has much in common with Henri Bergson's notion of living beings as affective "centers of indetermination." See Henri Bergson, *Matter and Memory*, trans. Nancy Margaret Paul and W. Scott Palmer (New York: Zone Books, 1991), 28–34.

9 Lyotard addresses this double functioning of the sign in "The Tensor." Like Guattari, Lyotard's point of departure is Freud's theory of the drives. Lyotard merely points out that the sign can operate within two (or presumably even more) economies—metonymic and metaphoric systems, but also affective ones: "It is at once a sign that creates meaning through divergence and opposition, and a sign that creates intensity through strength and singularity." Jean-François Lyotard, "The Tensor," trans. Seán Hand, in *The Lyotard Reader*, ed. Andrew Benjamin (Oxford: Blackwell, 1989), 11.

10 "[T]he work of art [...] is *a bloc of sensations, that is to say, a compound of percepts and affects*. Percepts are no longer perceptions; they are independent of a state of those who experience them. Affects are no longer feelings or affections; they go beyond the strength of those who undergo them. Sensations, percepts, and affects are beings whose validity lies in themselves and exceeds any lived." Gilles Deleuze and Félix Guattari, *What Is Philosophy?*, trans. Graham Burchill and Hugh Tomlinson (London: Verso, 1994), 164; italics in the original.

In their chapter on art in *What Is Philosophy?*, Deleuze and Guattari map out a theory and language of art outside of representation. I want to note here an interesting dovetailing of their theory with a kind of aporia that "The Social History of Art," and in particular T. J. Clark, finds itself/himself in. Suffice to say that Deleuze and Guattari's language—of movement, materials, and matter—is precisely the object of art history's secret desire and fear; a language of art that is no longer to do with signifiers and signifieds (poached, as Clark himself remarks, from film theory). Unfortunately, all materialist art historians eventually, and inevitably, hit an aporia, which, very briefly, goes like this: How to attend to the material object behind the ideological veils (the cultural readings/meanings) while still attending to the object's history? The problem arises because ideology and history are here synonymous. In a sense, "The Social History of Art," and art history in general, could not, cannot, put this language together: they are working within the horizon of signification. A language of material and matter would, for them, be a fetishization—an emptying out of meaning or of that trope of meaning: history. They would be guilty of the very ideological mystification that they are against. It is only within a different model or paradigm that a language of materials and matter "makes sense."

11 Paul de Man, "Literary History and Literary Modernity," in *Blindness and Insight: Essays in the Rhetoric of Contemporary Criticism* (London: Routledge, 1989), 148–49; italics in the original.

12 Massumi is useful in rethinking the relationship between the event (as intensity), and experience: "Although the realm of intensity that Deleuze's philosophy strives to conceptualise is transcendental in the sense that it is not directly accessible to experience, it is not transcendent, it is not

exactly outside experience either. It is immanent to it—always in it but not of it. Intensity and experience accompany one another, like two mutually presupposing dimensions, or like two sides of a coin. Intensity is immanent to matter and to events, to mind and to body and to every level of bifurcation composing them and which they compose." Hence, intensity for Massumi is indeed experienced "in the proliferations of levels of organisation it ceaselessly gives rise to, generates and regenerates, at every suspended moment." Massumi, "Autonomy of Affect," 226.

13 For a tracking of this oscillation, see the debates around allegory in the visual arts carried out in *October*, in particular Craig Owens, "The Allegorical Impulse: Towards a Theory of Postmodernism," *October*, no. 12 (1980): 67–86. And, most impressive, Stephen Melville, "Notes on the Reemergence of Allegory, the Forgetting of Modernism, the Necessity of Rhetoric, and the Conditions of Publicity in Art and Art Criticism," *October*, no. 19 (1981): 55–92.

14 See, for example, Andrew Benjamin, *The Plural Event: Descartes, Hegel, Heidegger* (London: Routledge, 1993). For another take on this problematic, especially in relation to Deleuze's project of thinking multiplicity, see Alain Badiou, *Deleuze: The Clamor of Being*, trans. Louise Burchill (Minneapolis: University of Minnesota Press, 1999).

15 For Deleuze and Guattari, art is "a zone of indetermination, of indiscernibility, as if things, beasts, and persons […] endlessly reach that point that immediately precedes their natural differentiation. This is what is called an affect. […] Life alone creates such zones where living beings whirl around, and only art can reach and penetrate them in its enterprise of cocreation." *What Is Philosophy?*, 173.

16 Badiou, *Deleuze*, 84n5.

17 Bergson, *Matter and Memory*, 101–2.

18 Gilles Deleuze and Félix Guattari, *A Thousand Plateaus: Capitalism and Schizophrenia*, trans. Brian Massumi (London: Athlone, 1994), 149–66.

19 Georges Bataille, *Prehistoric Painting: Lascaux or the Birth of Art*, trans. Austryn Wainhouse (London: Macmillan, 1980).

20 Jean-François Lyotard, *Peregrinations: Law, Form, Event* (New York: Columbia University Press, 1988), 18. In general, Lyotard tends to configure this unknown event in Kantian terms, specifically in relation to the sublime. As we shall see, there need not be recourse to the transcendent in order to allow for the possibility of a beyond to everyday experience.

21 Deleuze and Guattari, *What Is Philosophy?*, 181–82. John Rajchman has also written on this notion of the abstract, and on its difference to the more typical, one might say Greenbergian, notion of abstraction as reduction and purity. For Rajchman, abstraction must be understood as a realm of possibilities, of potentialities, prior to figuration. In order to paint, "one must come to see the surface not so much as empty or blank but rather as intense, where 'intensity' means filled with the unseen virtuality of other strange possibilities." John Rajchman, "Abstraction," in *Constructions* (Cambridge, MA: MIT Press, 1998), 61. The question of how to "paint outside force" is, according to Rajchman's reading of Deleuze, "the basic question of modernity." Ibid., 60.

22 This insight can be experienced through drugs, through meditation, through anything that, if only for a moment, dissolves the molar aggregate of our subjectivity.

23 As Deleuze and Guattari remark, the "principal strata binding human beings are the organism, significance and interpretation, and subjectification and subjection." *A Thousand Plateaus*, 134. It is the function of the following plateau of their book, "How to Make Yourself a Body without Organs," to offer strategies for destratification. This plateau might also be considered as a mapping of a series of experimental strategies for accessing the realm of affect. It is worth noting Deleuze and Guattari's warning here, which alerts readers against "wildly destratifying"—this can end merely in empty, botched bodies without organs (or worse). In fact, "you have to keep enough of the organism for it to reform each dawn; and you have to keep small supplies of significance and subjectification, if only to turn them against their own systems when circumstances demand it […]

and you have to keep small rations of subjectivity in sufficient quantity to enable you to respond to the dominant reality." Ibid., 160. See also my "In Violence: Three Case Studies against the Stratum," *Parallax* 6, no. 2 (2000): 115–21.

24 Gilles Deleuze, *Negotiations: 1972–1990*, trans. Martin Joughin (New York: Columbia University Press, 1995), 26.

25 Victor Burgin, *The End of Art Theory: Criticism and Postmodernity* (London: Macmillan, 1986), 147.

26 Theodor W. Adorno, *Aesthetic Theory*, trans. Christian Lenhardt (London: Routledge, 1984), 196.

27 Theodor W. Adorno, *Minima Moralia: Reflections on a Damaged Life*, trans. E. F. N. Jephcott (London: Verso, 1978), 247.

28 Gilles Deleuze, *Difference and Repetition*, trans. Paul Patton (London: Athlone Press, 1994), 211.

29 For a thorough working through of this logic of the real and the possible, the virtual and the actual, see Gilles Deleuze, *Bergsonism*, trans. Hugh Tomlinson and Barbara Habberjam (New York: Zone Books, 1991), 96–98.

30 As do philosophy, science and, as we have seen, prosthetic technologies. By altering our temporal and spatial registers new technology opens worlds previously invisible to us, but not worlds nonexistent. We can say something similar about pure mathematics: abstract equations as a way of actualizing events and processes that cannot be represented (indeed, this actualization is a form of problem solving).

31 As Massumi remarks: "It is the edge of the virtual, where it leaks into the actual, that counts. For that seeping edge is where potential, actually, is found." Massumi, "Autonomy of Affect," 236.

32 Félix Guattari, *Chaosmosis: An Ethico-Aesthetic Paradigm*, trans. Julian Pefanis and Paul Bains (Sydney: Power Institute of Fine Arts, 1995), 7.

33 Ibid.

34 For Deleuze and Guattari, philosophy is not a utopian pursuit in the sense of positing transcendent (and thus authoritarian) utopias. However, philosophy might be figured as utopian if we understand by this term immanent, revolutionary utopias. Indeed, for Deleuze and Guattari, political philosophy is this kind of utopian practice. It involves a "resistance to the present," and a creation of concepts that in itself "calls for a future form, for a new people that do not yet exist." Deleuze and Guattari, *What Is Philosophy?*, 108. Although not within the scope of this essay, a reading of Frankfurt School utopias via Deleuze and Guattari's notion of immanence would be an interesting and productive project. They themselves seem to have this in mind when they footnote the writings of Ernst Bloch in *What Is Philosophy?* (see page 224).

35 A good example of rethinking art away from the horizon of instrumental reason (and of the latter's critique) is Ronald Bogue, "Art and Territory," in *A Deleuzian Century?*, ed. Ian Buchanan (Durham, NC: Duke University Press, 1999), 265–69. Bogue, taking his lead from Deleuze's notion of the refrain, argues that bird song, as a kind of art practice, involves processes and movements of territorialization, deterritorialization, and reterritorialization. Which is to say that art is not, here, involved in a logic of the possible, but is to do with function: a function of deterritorialization.

36 Quoted in Stephen Bann, "Three Images for Kristeva: From Bellini to Proust," *Parallax* 4, no. 3 (1998): 69.

37 Bogue has outlined this "aesthetics of force," as he calls it, in relation to painting and, more interestingly, in relation to music (see "Gilles Deleuze: The Aesthetics of Force," in *Deleuze: A Critical Reader*). Bogue reads Deleuze as offering an "open system" of the arts where what is at stake is less a definition of art or any demarcation between the aesthetic and the nonaesthetic, but rather a general function of art as what "harnesses forces" (ibid., 268). This is particularly the case with painting, and of course Deleuze outlines this theory in relation to the paintings of Francis Bacon. However, music is also involved in forces. As Bogue remarks: "The basic function of the refrain is to territorialise forces, to regularise, control and encode the unpredictable world in regular patterns. But the refrain never remains purely closed and stable. Its emergence from the

chaotic flux is only provisional and its rhythms always issue forth to the cosmos at large" (ibid., 265). This larger function of deterritorialization is precisely a "line of flight" into the molecular. It is this—an affective line (and, I would argue, an aesthetic one)—that defines art.

38 Lyotard makes this exact point: "Today's art consists in exploring things unsayable and things invisible. Strange machines are assembled, where what we didn't have the idea of saying or the matter to feel can make itself heard and experienced." Jean-François Lyotard, "Philosophy and Painting in the Age of Their Experimentation: Contribution to an Idea of Postmodernity," trans. M. Minich Brewer and Daniel Brewer, in Benjamin, *The Lyotard Reader*, 190.

39 I attempt such a project, albeit briefly, in this essay's companion piece, "Writing on Art (Case Study: The Buddhist Puja)," *Parallax* 7, no. 4 (2001): 115–21.

I

A woman stands in the deep end of an empty and disused swimming pool. She wipes her face and stomach with her hands to clean away blood. Inside, she places her hands on the outstretched arm of a man who lifts her into the air and catches her when she falls. An eel breathes through its gills as it swims. The woman settles the eel in her arms and holds it against her body. When the woman swims she breathes out under water.[1]

This is how Jayne Parker's ten-minute film *The Pool* (1991) is described in the catalogue to her 2000–01 touring exhibition "Foxfire Eins."[2] The words, direct and factual like the film itself, recount a series of somewhat disconnected actions that could be described as ritualistic, even redemptive. For these actions (standing, wiping away blood, being lifted, holding, swimming, breathing out) seem to transform a traumatized and degraded space—the empty, rubble-strewn pool from the film's opening sequence—into a bountiful one: the clean, tiled, water-filled pool in which the woman swims, quickly backward and forward, in the final sequence. This sense of the ritualistic and apparently redemptive is not surprising. As film theorist A. L. Rees has noted, one of the traditions that Parker's work references is that of the psychodrama, which "grew as an avant-garde genre in the late silent-film era, as in the Surrealist films of Man Ray and Buñuel/Dalí."[3] In the psychodrama "a protagonist undergoes ritual tests of selfhood and identity—a struggle which must end either in death or rebirth."[4] In *The Pool*, however, and even though the woman's actions (performed by Parker) generally take center stage, this ritual-like activity seems to be orientated away from conventional, human-centered understandings of selfhood and identity toward broader, intercorporeal identifications with the nonhuman world and with the environment.

In *The Pool* this expansive, non-alienated dis-identification with anthropocentrism is evidenced particularly by formal and compositional means: not only by the woman's progressive attempts to move from the realm of earth and air (that which best supports human life) to the less hospitable realm of water, but also by her continued attempts to reorient her body along a horizontal rather than a vertical axis. In fact, horizontality is emphasized throughout the film, including in the way in which the camera, as witness, has been set up to frame what is on show. For instance, when the film opens with a single, pre-title establishing shot of the abandoned swimming pool, its tight, symmetrical framing accentuates the rectangular structure of its dilapidated rectangular base. Due to the framing, this image has the odd effect of also horizontalizing the screen on which it is shown. The sequence immediately following the titles (simple white text on a black background) shows the woman, Parker, standing in, then walking through, the disused swimming pool, her naked body bleeding from the nose. The first image we see of her, though, is a close-up of her torso, its proportions and positioning in relation to the screen exactly duplicating those of the pool in the opening sequence. In other words, her body is initially presented as if it too is a distressed horizontal plane, a plane upon which drops of blood begin to fall, one after the other, and, significantly, to accumulate. In the next sequence, Parker, now clothed, faces the camera and performs precise physical exercises with dancer Donald MacLeary, who repeatedly lifts her off the ground in a variety of vertical jumps and horizontal extensions. Here, a further motif consists of repeated shots of MacLeary's outstretched arm, which he offers to Parker as a horizontal support at the beginning of the horizontal lifts. (MacLeary, who has had a long career with the Royal Ballet, London, as principal dancer from 1959, as ballet master, and then répétiteur, would later perform with Lynn Seymour in Parker's 1997 film *The Reunion*.)

Horizontality is carried forward in the fourth sequence of *The Pool* in two intertwined ways: through the motions of the eel, filmed close up as it swims in a seemingly boundless expanse of dark water (actually, it is contained within an aquarium), and, more fundamentally, through the eel's own physiology. Suddenly though, in contrast to the eel's fluid movements, the surface texture of the footage changes, now appearing granular and degraded. It is also now that both the eel's fathomless, aquatic universe and the dimensions of the film itself are amplified by music. Max Eastley's haunting, agitated electro-acoustic composition breaks into what had, up to then, been a filmic atmosphere of near silence in which only natural, diegetic sounds could be heard. In the film's fifth sequence (Eastley's composition continues), Parker is again naked. She is holding the large, inert body of the eel—now out of its natural element—against her body, its elongated form stretched over the support created by her horizontal forearms. Then comes a momentary shot that is worth considering at some length: Parker and the eel are shown from further back, framed against a shallow, arched niche in a way that suggests further possible ritualistic associations. For instance, in this setting the pose suddenly recalls Christian iconography: the scene evokes a pietà, that is, a conventional image-type in which Mary, caught in what would appear to be a moment of cosmic failure, holds the dead (i.e., not-yet-resurrected) Christ's broken body in her arms. Indeed, in iconographic terms, the eel, which is an order of elongated fish, may be directly equated with Christ. (Christ was assigned the symbol of the fish by first-century Christians who wished to identify and gather with one another secretly. This was prudent within the treacherous political environment of the Roman Empire, in which their faith was deemed treasonous.)

Alternatively, if, due to its elongated form, the eel is taken to be a kind of serpent, other associations may also arise, most obviously with the biblical Fall of Man. Of special art-historical pertinence would be an association with *Laocoön and His Sons,* the imposing marble sculpture, which reputedly dates from the first or second century BCE, was excavated in Rome in 1506, and is now part of the Vatican Collection. It shows Laocoön, Trojan priest of Greek mythology, and his two sons in mortal combat with a huge serpent sent in vengeance by Apollo to slay them—a story, incidentally, that is precisely the inverse of the founding narrative of Christianity, just referenced, where it is God manifested in human form, namely Christ, who dies in order to redeem otherwise irrevocably disordered and estranged human beings. *Laocoön and His Sons* has, of course, been discussed extensively within the history of art, particularly in the eighteenth century, when art history was in the early stages of being established as a recognized academic discipline, and specifically by thinkers who were contributing to this quest by trying to identify essential distinctions between the visual arts on the one hand, and other "high" cultural practices (notably poetry and music) on the other. Thus in the 1755 *Reflections on the Imitation of Greek Works in Painting and Sculpture*, the art historian Johann Joachim Winckelmann focuses on the contrast between Virgil's textual account of the struggle in which Laocoön is presented emitting "terrible screams," and that of the sculpture in which he figures as "a great and composed soul even in the midst of passion."[5] As I will show, a sense of emotional restraint or reticence also marks Parker's performance in *The Pool*. Winckelmann's reflections were both developed and critiqued a few years later by the philosopher and critic Gotthold Ephraim Lessing. In his 1766 essay "Laocoön: An Essay on the Limits of Painting and Poetry," Lessing explicitly challenges Horace's well-known dictum, *ut pictura poesis* (as is painting so is poetry), by insisting on important relationships of difference between the operations of image and word within high art. In so doing, he examined the relative possibilities and limitations within each of those creative forms for the expression of intense emotion. These questions have remained central to art history and visual culture, and recur throughout this essay.

In *The Pool*'s final sequence, Parker is immersed in water. Shot from below, by a camera that is also beneath the water, she swims back and forth with speed and concentration, her body stretching and contracting, head underwater, eyes closed. The water itself swirls and gushes against and over her body, its sounds now steadily overtaking until entirely replacing Eastley's music. Then, for a moment, the horizontal force of Parker's movements is suspended. Verticality temporarily reasserts itself as her body suddenly hovers in the water and reaches upward for air. But when the film ends a moment later, she has renewed her efforts and started swimming again.

In an interview, Parker said that at issue in many of her films, including this one, is the phenomenon of "witnessing myself trying to do things that are difficult."[6] She notes that they also frequently have to do with a quest for transformation. But if the film does, in this way, convey a sense of the psychodramatic or ritualistic, it nonetheless resists easy interpretation—Parker herself has remarked that she has difficulty saying what, precisely, her films are about.[7] But what is apparent throughout *The Pool* is the way in which the film conveys a strong sense of enlargement, even shift, in terms of what the human body's characteristics, intimate relations, and physical or environmental extensions could consist of. And there is, of course, a strong sense of parity between the different levels of bodily or physical experience at issue—the woman's, the eel's—and the characteristics of the environment; a parity that perhaps should not be interpreted as only or merely metaphorical. Returning to the matter of the woman's repeated entrances into horizontality, it is noteworthy that these are never entrances into a posture traditionally associated with sleep or death. Instead, horizontality is tied to experiences that are intensely attentive, active, and alive as much as they are also determinedly surrendered to certain less than hospitable surroundings or situations.

A second observation about *The Pool*, one already intimated, is that its ritualistic character, and its depiction of what could be described as intercorporeal life force, are undergirded, not undermined, by the film's restrained, objective qualities. These objective qualities apply to certain other films of hers from this period; according to Rees, together with Parker's film *K* (1989), *The Pool* marks a transition from her earlier work in this regard. Parker began filmmaking in 1979 while studying sculpture at Canterbury College of Art. As well as having certain affinities with feminist filmmakers and performance artists from the 1960s and '70s, Rees positions her among a new generation of artists who were working in the wake of structuralist filmmaking (with its materially orientated, nonnarrative focus), but who were directing their vision in new ways. For instance, he describes Parker's films as "cast in an almost symbolist visual language."[8] Nonetheless, he adds, they also resist "the impositions of the word and of description."[9] He continues, "They deal with sensations and ideas at the borderline of naming, or maybe with namelessness itself."[10] Analogously, although *The Pool* does gesture toward a narrative of sorts, and might be seen to have a beginning, middle, and end, its structure is so abbreviated and full of juxtapositions that it could just as easily be understood as the first part of a longer, as yet unavailable sequence of scenes. Furthermore, in spite of the fact that, like in her earlier works, Parker again appears as a performer in her own work, *The Pool* was made in an impersonal mode. For instance, she was now no longer filmed by friends or colleagues, "by people who knew her [...] which [had] led to the special, delicate and beautifully observed quality" of earlier pieces, but by professionals.[11] Furthermore, the spaces in which these later films were shot were more objective: "From now on, she used more public and even anonymous locations—bare studios, swimming pools, each of them precise but not locatable in the same way as before."[12] Crucially, the objective mode as it is presented here does not seem to be associated with mastery but, again, with attempts to discover a center of relational gravity that is not anthropocentric.

The implicit power of the impersonal, anonymous, and objective also characterizes the work of Rosalind Nashashibi, who belongs to a later generation of British artist-filmmakers. Born in 1973 in London, and having studied at Sheffield Hallam University and Glasgow School of

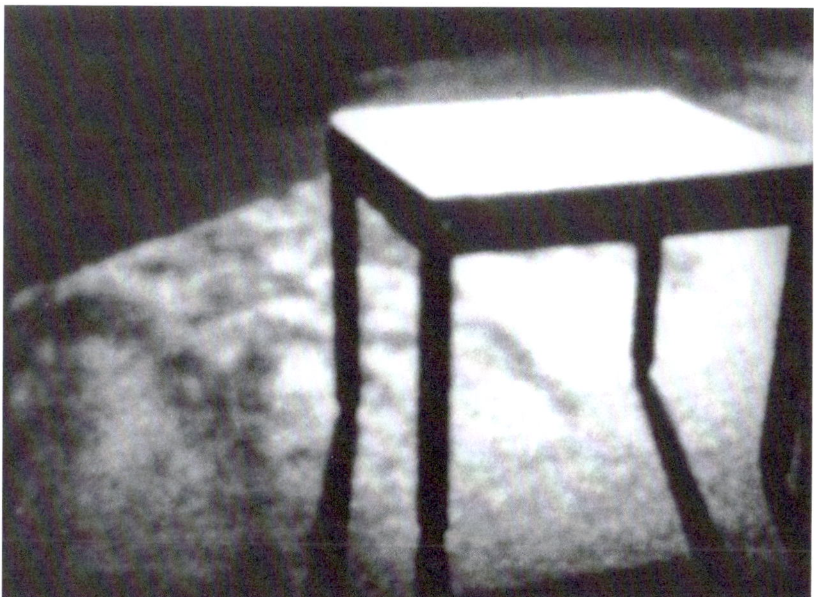

STILL FROM: ROSALIND NASHASHIBI, *STONE AND TABLE*, 1994. 4 MINS, BLACK-AND-WHITE 16-MM FILM LOOP. COPYRIGHT ROSALIND NASHASHIBI. COURTESY ROSALIND NASHASHIBI AND LUX, LONDON.

Art, Nashashibi began to exhibit her work nationally and internationally in late 1990s, winning the prestigious, now-defunct Beck's Futures prize in 2003. As with Parker's *The Pool*, Nashashibi's *Stone and Table* (1994–2000), a 4 minute, 16 mm silent film loop, could be said to have three protagonists. Not a woman, a man, and an eel, but a stone, a bare, unattended table—the camera focuses on each in turn, in what appears to be an unspecified outdoor space—and, in a lesser role, significantly, the trace of an unseen person in the form of a shadow that, every now and then, passes over these scenes. In other words, the film's main actors are two inanimate objects. Yet both are made to appear full of life, or life force. This is again achieved through formal means. With its black-and-white surface appearing scratched and faded, as if a remnant of celluloid from long ago, *Stone and Table* runs at only three frames per second, rather than the usual twenty-four. This gives not only the film, but also the filmed objects, a pulse, an active as well as a provisional and open, even environmental, character. Through this process, and through the camera's often extreme close-up perspectives, the stone becomes a universe of curves and miniscule, textured crevices; of holes within holes, and shadows within shadows. The film's regular, rhythmic beat also seems to transform the stone into an organic, heart-like thing. Likewise, the table to which the film cuts about halfway through, with its rectangular surface catching the light as it casts simple, gridded patterns under a shifting sun, is presented not as an object of everyday use (like the pool at the beginning of Parker's film, Nashashibi's table has an abandoned quality), but as a matrix of lines and planes in which material and immaterial realms intersect. These ever shifting compositions draw us in, and in this sense the film makes us aware of the nature of our own seeing. At times, we might also find ourselves thinking associatively. Despite the archaic feel of the scenes before us, the table's bright, rectangular surface glinting in the sun cannot but remind us of that similarly glowing icon of modernity that is literally in front of us: the cinematic screen. In this way, through purely visual means, a powerful juxtaposition is set up in this part of *Stone and Table* between a pictured pseudo-screen that seems to await projection as our internal image repertoires are activated, and the actual screen we are watching, upon which things show themselves with, as I will argue, a liberating unconcern for our interests, agendas, or ideas. They are there and we, like those fleeting human shadows, are much less permanent passersby. Once again, to repeat, the film seems to emphasize a strong sense of agency located not in subjects but in things and in the relationship between things.

So what are we to make of these films more broadly? Beyond their strong visual aesthetics in which gestures, surface qualities, and the interplay of shapes, forms, and textures are foregrounded, and despite those moments when possible symbolic or metaphorical associations may be proffered and picked up, they seem to have no explicit message to convey. Are these works, therefore, just anachronistic reversions to a mode of art-for-art's-sake irrelevance that the politicized work of the mid-twentieth century was so critical of? Are they apolitical? Irresponsibly so? This is certainly a charge that was directed by some at a later work by Nashashibi: her six-minute, nonnarrative film *Dahiet al Bareed, District of the Post Office* (2002). Shot close to a military checkpoint, in a Palestinian neighborhood outside of Jerusalem—the latter had been designed in part by Nashashibi's grandfather, Saeb Nashashibi, in 1956, as a utopian suburb for employees of the Palestinian post office—the film would seem to demand some kind of embedded politicized commentary. But we are given none of this. Instead, the camera simply records sequences of everyday life: men talking in a barber's shop, children playing with apparent enjoyment among ruins, the detritus of conflict, litter. Indeed, since the turn of the twenty-first century, this kind of approach to the moving image and to subject matter has developed into the genre now known as "video painting."[13] Here, the filmed action unfolds before a static camera and is presented without later edits. There is thus a strong nonnarrative aspect to this work, a refusal to inject meaning or offer explanation, and extreme openness to incident. Whatever happens to occur within the frame, or passes by it, is included.

II

"Out of the anti-aestheticism of postmodernism has emerged a renewed interest in aesthetics."[14] So writes Barbara Bolt in her 2011 book *Heidegger Reframed*. This renewed interest, increasingly evident in art practices from the 1990s, has at least two variants. One variant relates to the kind of work just described, to which I will return. The other, and arguably the more dominant variant, was most famously identified and discussed by the curator Nicolas Bourriaud in his book *Relational Aesthetics*, first published in French in 1998. At issue here are diverse art practices that seemed to share the following characteristic: directly or indirectly, as with much postmodern and indeed much earlier twentieth-century art, they all challenged the (supposedly) elitist idea of the artwork as an object of art-for-art's-sake contemplation, or as an object of consumption or exchange within the circuits of capital. Against these tendencies, they attempted to reinstate the social, political, and ethical efficacy of art. But they did so without resorting to the oppositional or didactic message-based strategies of much twentieth-century and contemporary activist or protest art. Instead, as Bourriaud saw it, artists like Rirkrit Tiravanija, Philippe Parreno, Vanessa Beecroft, Maurizio Cattelan, and Christine Hill were evolving a new understanding of the aesthetic that was grounded in "interactive, user-friendly and relational concepts."[15]

The first example of a relational artwork cited by Bourriaud in *Relational Aesthetics* was a dinner organized by Tiravanija in a collector's house, for which the artist left him "all the ingredients required to make a Thai soup."[16] Analogously, the cover of his book shows an installation shot of Tiravanija's 1996 exhibition, "Untitled, 1996 (One Revolution per Minute)" at Le Consortium in Dijon, which reveals an informal setup involving tables, benches, chairs, food and drink, and piles of books; audiences are invited to make themselves at home, and engage. Of note, however, within the context of this essay, is that in works by Tiravanija—and arguably this is a uniting characteristic of all or most of the art gathered by Bourriaud under the designation "relational aesthetics"—there is a sense that although objects, often nonart objects of different kinds, play important roles, their ultimate function is to facilitate provisional, if not longer term, shifts in human sociality. Bourriaud describes work of this kind, and the space in which it is exhibited, as a "social *interstice*."[17] Such works provide "free areas" and "time spans" that enable us to experiment and improvise with the ways we interrelate outside of the preestablished or already scripted "communication zones" that—he says—regulate and diminish our everyday interactions.[18] Here, then, expanded notions of human intersubjectivity take center stage. These may, in turn, have an impact on how subjectivity itself is conceptualized and experienced. But such questions do not seem to be a particular point of focus. Rather, the importance of received notions of human subjectivity is intensified as objects, and the events in which they participate, are put to work in the service of human life—albeit within the context of a broad emancipatory project. In Bourriaud's words: "It is evident that today's art is carrying on this fight, by coming up with perceptive, experimental, critical and participatory models, veering in the direction indicated by Enlightenment philosophers, Proudhon, Marx, the Dadaists and Mondrian."[19] He continues: "If opinion is striving to acknowledge the legitimacy and interest of these experiments, this is because they are no longer presented like the precursory phenomena of an inevitable historical evolution. Quite to the contrary, they appear fragmentary and isolated, like orphans of an overall view of the world bolstering them with the clout of an ideology."[20]

Bourriaud's text is an important instance of noticing patterns within that milieu of fragmentation so that phenomena within the arts that would otherwise pass by unnoticed can be attended to, reflected upon, talked about, and acted upon—a turn to the power of small gestures. But my interests are with that body of post-1990s aesthetically oriented work that is at first sight more conventional than the work of Tiravanija and others referred to by Bourriaud. Certainly Parker's and Nashashibi's works are more directly concerned with the effects of form and materiality. Certainly, as noted, it is harder for their political, social, or ethical value to be determined. And, indeed, as film or video pieces they can more easily and uncritically be absorbed into the art market (although it is also true that this market has long been adept at accommodating and making money from immaterial phenomena and fleeting experiences as well). Nonetheless, I argue that this second body of aesthetically oriented work is more philosophically and existentially radical than those works foregrounded by Bourriaud. Why? Because by focusing attention on the lifeworlds of objects, and on inter*corporeality* instead of inter*subjectivity,* a powerful sense of agency is opened up that does not appear to be immediately directed to, or in service of, purely human concerns. Instead of generating "interactive, user-friendly and relational concepts," the aesthetics associated with these works call into question the anthropocentric assumptions that habitually undergird everyday life, thought, and action—an anthropocentrism that relational aesthetics also affirms. Hence the title of my essay, "Intending Objects and Signs '*Which Have No Meaning*,'" which is drawn from the final chapter of Kaja Silverman's book *World Spectators*, "The Language of Things."[21] I will discuss this later. But in order to start considering the importance and impact of, for want of a better expression, the stubbornly object-generated aesthetics I am interested in, I turn to Martin Heidegger's fervent *rebuttal* of aesthetics: his 1938 lecture "The Age of the World Picture."[22] As will become apparent, however, his objection is to "the modern [anthropocentric or subject-centered] tradition of philosophical 'aesthetics,'"[23] which remains dominant today and to which Bourriaud's relational aesthetics, too, remain indebted.

In his essay, Heidegger's argument against aesthetics occurs within the context of a broader critique of the modern age. He defines the latter with reference to five "essential phenomena": (1) science, (2) machine technology, (3) the event of art's moving into the purview of aesthetics, (4) culture as the realization of the highest human values, and, finally, (5) the loss of the gods. Accompanying all of these phenomena, he claims, is a newly formulated and dangerously reductive conception of mankind in which "man becomes the primary and only real *subiectum* [...] the relational center of that which is as such."[24]

The modern has, of course, been differently located and theorized according to academic discipline and thinker. Art historians conventionally associate modernity in art with the period spanning the later nineteenth to the mid-twentieth centuries. Some philosophical thinkers, by contrast, have associated it with the rise of Socratic and Platonic thought, and still others with the rise of humanism and secularism during the

Renaissance. Informing Heidegger's conception of the modern age, however, was the paradigm-shifting metaphysics of Descartes, which set out to achieve intellectual clarity and control through its radical dualism and its representationalist logic: the idea that reality can be established only upon the foundations of, and according to intellectual projections from, the *cogito ergo sum*, the "I think, therefore I am." As Heidegger put it, with Descartes "what it is to be is for the first time defined as the objectiveness of representing, and truth is first defined as the certainty of representation."[25] At issue, in other words, was a newly inaugurated worldview very different to that of either the ancient Greeks or the medieval schoolmen. For here, reputedly, was a world reformulated purely in terms of man, one in which Protagoras's pre-Socratic claim that "man is the measure of all things" had been taken to an extreme. The world—including the world of other people—was reconceptualized as mechanistic, predictable, definable, and controllable. Not only was it taken to be at the disposal of human plans and projects, conversely it was also taken to be the outcome of them.

Significantly, then, the world became, in Heidegger's terms, not merely something to be understood as *manipulandum* or resource, but a world understood as *picture*. Here, crucially—and as already implied—the word "picture [*Bild*]" now meant not a picture of the world but "the structured image [*Gebild*] that is the creature of man's producing which represents and sets before."[26] Within the process of such "producing," to reiterate, "man contends for the position in which he can be that particular being who gives the measure and draws up the guidelines for everything that is."[27] "Man puts himself in the picture [...] he stands over what is. He becomes the representative [*der Repräsentant*] of that which is," Heidegger wrote.[28] And again: "The fundamental event of the modern age is the conquest of the world as picture."[29] Clearly then, in keeping with his broader philosophical project, Heidegger's position also problematized humanism—certainly humanism as it came to be inflected through

Cartesianism. While humanism was a direction already foreshadowed in Platonic thought in the fourth century BCE, according to Heidegger it redefined and reasserted itself in the seventeenth century: "It is no wonder that humanism first arises where the world becomes picture."[30]

So what, then, of the relationship between the negative notion of "world picture" as set out in "The Age of the World Picture," and the notion of the (true) work of art as Heidegger understood it during this period? This is a crucial question, because it was while "The Age of the World Picture" was first being devised that a culture was emerging in Weimar Germany in which the mindset that was at once the producer and product of that "age" was being activated toward definite nationalistic, that is, xenophobic and ideological, ends. Significantly, too, within this context, questions about art and aesthetics had become high on the political agenda and were being played out not just within German artistic and intellectual circles, but within the public realm. After all, a year earlier, in 1937, two notoriously opposed art exhibitions had opened in Munich. On the one hand, there was the "Entartete Kunst" (Degenerate Art) exhibition, where diverse modernist artworks, considered to be anti-German, were displayed for public ridicule. Works by such artists as Max Beckmann, Marc Chagall, Otto Dix, George Grosz, Johannes Itten, and Wassily Kandinsky were included. Over a four-month period it was visited by around two million people, and during 1938 and 1939 a scaled-down version toured other cities in Germany and Austria. On the other hand, there was the Great German Art Exhibition held at the newly opened House of German Art—visited by a much smaller number of people—where works by artists officially sanctioned by the governing National Socialists were celebrated. At issue in each case were not only questions of content, but also, and especially, of "good" versus "bad" form with respect to how people, things, and situations were portrayed. These exhibitions and Heidegger's writing shared fervently antimodernist sentiments. But as indicated, his particular antimodernist critique in "The Age of the World Picture" was of a different order.

In the lecture "The Origin of the Work of Art," which Heidegger first wrote and delivered between 1935 and 1936, he made his (non-representationalist) views on art explicit.[31] Art, he said, is that particular place of openness, that "clearing" within given historical contexts, where "what-is," or where Being, can reveal itself on its own terms, according to its own specific modes of disclosure/concealment. The significance of this disclosure (*aletheia*) was that it in turn impacted how historical communities come to understand the world and live in it. In the words of Iain Thomson, for Heidegger, art at its highest "works inconspicuously to establish, maintain, and transform humanity's historically variable sense of what is and what matters."[32] I will return to this notion of inconspicuousness later.

The problem with Cartesianism, however, was that its aims and methods closed down these spaces of appearance. As Heidegger put it, it had repositioned art "into the purview of aesthetics." As such, "the art work becomes the object of mere subjective experience, and [...] consequentially art is considered to be the expression of human life."[33] A fundamental reversal had taken place in which art's role was now to affirm and consolidate the subject in his or her subjectivity, plans, projects, and projections; to take that subject where he or she wants to go. Art was not in the service of truth, but, as noted earlier, in the service of human life. With a particular relevance to questions of meaning, Thomson notes that, in the "basic aesthetic approach to art" to which Heidegger is opposed, "art objects are implicitly understood as meaningful expressions of artists' lives that are capable of eliciting particularly intense or meaningful experiences in viewing subjects."[34]

This broad understanding of art has by now become so normalized that Heidegger's objections to it may seem difficult to grasp. He is adamant, however, that it be overturned—though not necessarily by going down the anti-art routes often chosen by other critics of aesthetics and its values, in which qualities associated either with the everyday (the idea of "low" rather than "high" or fine art) or with the abject might be foregrounded. For here, conventional aesthetic values still hold sway; they have merely been inverted. The challenge is rather to elude the hold of such conventions altogether by investigating "what other centers of relationship" there might be.[35] But *if* the self-referential impositions of modern subjectivity are to be dislodged—and *if* art is to regain potency as more than merely representative or expressive of human perceptions, feelings, thoughts, and values—much else must also be rethought, not least the nature and location of thought, and the nature and location of agency. Indeed, at their highest, these must be understood to operate outside of the domain of human planning, devising, systematizing, projecting, and mastering. Likewise the world of things, and other people, must be understood to operate and interact in ways that may acknowledge us, but that also remain resistant to human subjectivity, sometimes leaving it—that is, us—out of the loop.

At this point, therefore, it is worth considering a fleeting metaphor (is it also more than that?) that appears near the end of "The Age of the World Picture." Heidegger writes that when practices of "planning, devising, systematizing, projecting, and mastering" are assiduously pursued (and this is precisely what he is critiquing), they inevitably over-reach themselves, departing from the realm of calculability into that of incalculability. This realm of incalculability he describes, metaphorically, as an "invisible shadow"—invisible, that is, to the calculating mind. Nonetheless, this "shadow" exerts a disturbing force, causing the world-as-picture to lose its consistency and bearings, the world as a self-showing entity to be reanimated, and, in Heidegger's terms, the apprehension of truth to be possible again. "Man brings into play his unlimited power for the calculating, planning, and molding of all things," writes Heidegger, and continues:

> But as soon as the gigantic in planning and calculating and adjusting and making secure shifts over out of the quantitative and becomes a special quality, then what is gigantic, and what can seemingly always

be calculated completely, becomes, precisely through this, incalculable. This becoming incalculable remains the invisible shadow that is cast around all things everywhere when man has been transformed into *subiectum* and the world into picture.

By means of this shadow the modern world extends itself out into a space withdrawn from representation and so lends to the incalculable the determinateness peculiar to it, as well as a historical uniqueness. This shadow, however, points to something else, which it is denied to us of today to know. But man will never be able to experience and ponder this that is denied so long as he dawdles about in the mere negating of the age. The flight into tradition, out of a combination of humility and presumption, can bring about nothing in itself other than self-deception and blindness in relation to the historical moment.[36] Finally, therefore: "Man will know, i.e., carefully safeguard into its truth, that which is incalculable, only in creative questioning and shaping out of the power of genuine reflection. Reflection transports the man of the future into the 'between' in which he belongs to Being and yet remains a stranger amid that which is."[37]

At the level of metaphor, Heidegger's "invisible shadow" in "The Age of the World Picture" stands for at least three things. First, as noted, it stands for the unexpected by-product of a process that thinks itself to be autonomous, subject to absolute regulation, and unlimited in its scope. Second, it stands for that which ordinarily escapes rational apprehension (it is a realm of apparent concealment and muteness, resistant and unreadable) but is, in fact, ubiquitous within modernity. Third, it stands for a precise and situated revelatory power associated, here, not with light but with darkness, a precise and situated revelatory power to which it is vital we respond—even though this power is not necessarily, or only, directed toward us. For there is an important sense in which its most fundamental effect must be to estrange us from, and within, what is. It does so positionally and temporally, and therefore also intellectually, emotionally, and imaginatively. Note Heidegger's reference in this regard to an understanding of "genuine reflection" as that which "transports the man of the future into the 'between' in which he belongs to Being and yet remains a stranger amid that which is." It does so, however, in order to better embed us, perceptively and actively, within the particularities of our own historical here-and-now, and—crucially—up against the specific obstacles that are at issue. (Up against that which is "denied to us of today to know," for instance.) These are all themes and orientations that Silverman does much to open up. They are also conveyed in and through the works by Parker and Nashashibi, in which the object-generated and intercorporeal aesthetics that I am lauding as foundational to being are compellingly demonstrated. Here, art is that which enables us to enter into this often disregarded state of affairs, one which we may not be able to comprehend, but whose presence we nonetheless register.

Indeed, given that the artworks I have chosen to focus on in this essay foreground intercorporeality and the agency of objects, I would like to remain a little longer with the notion, just identified, of the "invisible shadow" in its revelatory mode. As suggested earlier, this understanding may best be developed if we remember that, as well as being an apt metaphor for the incalculable—since both phenomena may be associated with that which cannot be grasped—the shadow as a visual phenomenon is also a literal visible marker of that which is profoundly concrete and present. Not only do shadows point to the thereness and agency of light, they also testify to the objectness, the thereness, of things. In other words, it is precisely by means of this most intangible of phenomena that the tangibility, and therefore also the resistance, of the world is most forcibly asserted. This doubled characteristic of the shadow, its connection with both the ungraspable and the concrete, suggests that incalculability and material reality are best not thought of as opposed—a fact that has been well understood, ironically, within a visual tradition that has itself often been described as highly rationalized: illusionistic art making. The use of shadow, after all, is a principle means whereby illusionistic paintings and, later, photographs and films accomplish their extraordinary visual transformations of two dimensions into three. Take by way of example the instructions on this topic in Leon Battista Alberti's pioneering treatise *On Painting* from 1435. Here, alongside the proper application of linear perspective and a correct understanding of proportion—best accomplished with the aid of various mechanical devices[38]—a crucial role is accorded to the play of light and shade, that is, to the artist's use of white and black pigments to modify colored ones and thus produce convincingly modeled depictions of physical objects.[39]

> I agree that a wide range and variety of colours contribute greatly to the beauty and attraction of a painting. But I would prefer learned painters to believe that the greatest art and industry are concerned with the disposition of white and black, and that all skill and care should be used in correctly placing these two. Just as the incidence of light and shade makes it apparent where surfaces become convex or concave, or how much any part slopes and turns this way or that, so the combination of white and black achieves what the Athenian painter Nicias was praised for, and what the artist must above all desire: that the things he paints should appear in maximum relief.[40]

And again, a little later: "But as regards the representation of light with white and of shadow with black, I advise you to devote particular study to those surfaces that are clothed in light or shade. *You can very well learn from Nature and from objects themselves.*"[41]

These points concerning the determination to accord a leading epistemological role to the natural world and the object world (of which, of course, we are also a part) are worth underlining. For, as already indicated, one of the themes traversing this essay concerns an important distinction between the mimetic orientation that is at issue in this relationship—also embedded within the photographic and cinematic— and the kind of representational thinking to which Heidegger was opposed. This mimetic attitude—which is also enacted in the ritualistic intimacies of Parker's performance in *The Pool*—is not an attempt at mastery, but an attitude of attentiveness toward, submission to, and connection with nature-as-teacher. The imitation of nature draws us out of our own frames of reference and into the lived experience of otherness; into, indeed, a condition in which otherness not only discovers its own dimensions and forms of interaction, but is also able to replicate itself according to its own differential logics and rhetorics—a theme I will continue to develop in the next section of this essay. Admittedly, given the anti-illusionism that has been so prevalent within much modern and contemporary art practice and theory, this defense of mimesis may be somewhat controversial. But it has also received considerable critical support in places. One such place is another twentieth-century critique of instrumental reason, and of calculation as a means of dominating external and internal nature: Theodor W. Adorno's *Aesthetic Theory*. Published posthumously in 1970, we find in *Aesthetic Theory* the claim that only a mimetic relationship to nature can free us from the aggressive drive at the center of humanist subjectivity.

Returning our focus to the shadow, we might note another crucial way in which this particular image type contrasts with the notion of *Gebild* that Heidegger problematized. At issue now is the shadow's status as a natural picture, a picture that is produced, without human aid, as a result of the interaction of light with one or more objects intersecting its course. Within the art-historical tradition, the cast shadow was famously regarded as the origin of depiction in general. To cite Alberti again: "Quintillian believed that the earliest painters used to draw around shadows made by the sun, and the art eventually grew by a process of additions. Some say that an Egyptian Philocles and a certain Cleanthes were among the first inventors of this art."[42] The significance of photography, of course, was that it introduced a way of fixing these "drawings." In any case, we see again that this natural picturing (of which, at a fundamental, material level photography and the cinematic are types) evokes an objectivity, understood as a quality of receptiveness and submission to natural processes. This is crucial, since the perceptual world of things and other people made available in this way is much richer than the realm of our own conceptions and projections, which consistently tend toward the reductive, repetitive, and homogeneous. The notion of the shadow as a natural picture and therefore, in Heideggerian terms, a place of self-showing, also has particular affinities with the role—and the metaphor—of the darkroom in pre-digital photography as precisely such a place of disclosure. As noted earlier, in terms of its production as well as its content, Nashashibi's *Stone and Table* seems to point, in part, to these archaic image-making histories and their associations. Relevant too, of course, is the association made in Walter Benjamin's writing between photography and that other illuminating realm of darkness, the "optical unconscious."[43] Here, then, is a productive, un-Heideggerian connection between technology and *aletheia*.

III

When challenging the Cartesian *subiectum* and its worldview by investing agency in objects, it is paramount that the outcome is not simply a world turned upside down where power relations have been simply reversed. It is equally important that this object-generated agency, and the aesthetics associated with it, are not interpreted as self-referential or self-enclosed. As indicated previously, intercorporeality must be a foundational reality here, and flowing from it an ethics in which the world of objects and of others plays a legitimate role in terms of revealing *what is*, rather than being oriented toward what humanity, understood as *subiectum*, might wish or project (or, indeed, deny to be the case).

The dynamics and possibilities of intercorporeality, some of which have already been opened up in this essay, may be considered further with reference to three key ideas found in Silverman's writing. The first two are the notions of "intending objects" and "signs '*which have no meaning.*'" The third concept is that of the communication, or "correspondence" of forms, found in the collaborative work of one of Silverman's main interlocutors, literary theorist Leo Bersani.[44]

The notion of "intending objects," as Silverman discusses it, is drawn specifically from the later writing of Hannah Arendt but is, more broadly, a phenomenological concept. This is worth emphasizing, since phenomenology is characteristically defined as a philosophical position that takes subjectivity, and subjective experience, as its starting point, and as its only sphere of competence. This characterization is often used to disqualify phenomenological investigations from having a wider importance or impact. Certainly, such an understanding would seem to make it uniquely ill-equipped to challenge the concept and ascendency of the *subiectum* identified by Heidegger (himself a leading phenomenologist) as a core problem for dominant Western, and increasingly global, modes of thought and action.

The concept of intentionality is, however, central to phenomenological thought. In other words, rather than prioritizing a supposedly self-enclosed and autonomous subjective state (such as Descartes's *cogito ergo sum*), phenomenology's starting point is an already intercorporeal scene, in which the "I think" is always already directed toward other things and situations, and intentionality is always multivalent and multidirectional. Furthermore, we can speak not only of intending subjects, but also of intending objects. In the section of "The Language of Things" subtitled "Intending Objects," Silverman writes as follows:

> Whether we locate intentionality at the site of consciousness, the unconscious, or language, we are accustomed to thinking of it as something specific to the human psyche. The category of an "intending object" is consequently one to which we are likely to accede only so long as it designates a human being. However, early in *The Life of the Mind* Arendt makes it clear that this category is at least for her all-inclusive, one which includes even inanimate, dead, and man-made

substances. She also encourages us to locate intentionality in a very surprising place: in what might be called "brute materiality."[45]

The determination of phenomenology to focus on the intercorporeal structures of intentionality is crucial because it reconfigures our usual understandings of the character of communication and relationship. As I will show, turning to the theme with which Silverman's *World Spectators* ends, ultimately, the intercorporeal structures of intentionality reconfigure our usual understandings of the character of love—a theme that also bears on the history of art since, returning to myths of origin, a classical account recorded in the work of Pliny claims that the art of drawing began when, in remembrance of her departing lover, the Corinthian maid Dibutade outlined his shadow on the wall of her father's tiling studio. In their discussions of these relational matters, and although Silverman and Bersani share what Silverman has described as a commitment to "write constantly against the self—against mastery and power,"[46] both proceed along somewhat different trajectories.

At certain points, Silverman's understanding of intentionality and intercorporeality in "The Language of Things" appears to differ from the non-subject-centered existential and ethical orientation I am attempting to champion in this essay. For instance, she describes intending objects as objects that are very specifically directed toward human beings, giving themselves to be seen, and ultimately to be loved, not just by us, but in and through us. She refers, within this context, to an aspiration of the animal or thing "beyond what has been existentially given [...] its aspiration to complete itself within us."[47] This theme continues in a later section, "Letting the Landscape Speak Itself in Us," in which she turns to phenomenologist Maurice Merleau-Ponty's 1945 essay "Cézanne's Doubt" in which he cited Cézanne's reflection on his own experiences as a painter: "The landscape thinks itself in me and I am its consciousness."[48] But Silverman's apprehending subject is not the same as the *subiectum* critiqued by Heidegger. On the contrary, her apprehending subject is above all a receptor, a "recipient of appearance,"[49] and as such a zone of openness that cannot but also be altered in some way by the apprehension—cannot but experience his or her sense of self as being disturbed, rearticulated, or redistributed, in the encounter. Nonetheless, a certain anthropocentrism does still seem to be at issue here. For his part, Bersani takes a somewhat different position. In his discussions he is interested in relations in which "the human itself has no ontological priority."[50] Again, while Bersani and Silverman agree that, for all the human and nonhuman actors involved in a particular encounter, dissolutions of identity and coherence are part and parcel of the intercorporeal structures of intentionality—this understanding was also embedded, visually and compositionally, in the films of Parker and Nashashibi discussed earlier—Silverman connects these dissolutions with experiences of loss whereas Bersani does not. He refers instead to "a pleasure in losing or dissolving the self that is in no way equated with loss, but comes rather through rediscovering the self outside the self."[51] At issue, he says, "is a kind of spatial, anonymous narcissism."[52]

If divestitures of identity are key to the kinds of intercorporeal sociality in which Bersani and Silverman are both, albeit somewhat differently, interested, so too is the relinquishment of certain inherited, anthropocentric, and predominantly language- or concept-based notions of meaningfulness. Concerning this, Bersani makes reference to the impact of what he calls the "enigmatic signifier," that which is experienced in everyday life as a call, a primordial mode of address, that we cannot understand, that overwhelms us, and which we may therefore repress. (This may be seen to recall Heidegger's "The Age of the World Picture," and the way in which that "invisible shadow," by means of which "the modern world extends itself out into a space withdrawn from representation" is also repressed within modernity.) Analogously, Silverman turns to the writing of the twentieth-century sociologist, anthropologist, and philosopher Roger Caillois, and specifically to his "signs *which have no meaning*,"[53] a concept that is at first glance nonsensical.

We are not always in possession of the key by means of which to access a sign's meaning. Therefore, certain signs do not speak to us. Nevertheless, when face to face with a sign, we are always sure that meaning is somehow "there," even if hidden or buried. This is because our everyday way of thinking about a sign is precisely as something within which meaning "resides." What does it mean to refer to a form or a pattern as a sign when it is devoid even of this semantic latency? And how can we "read" signs which do not mean?[54]

It is not a provocation to become immersed in meaninglessness that is the issue for Silverman here, just as it was not for Bersani above. Instead, it is a question of becoming immersed in non-anthropocentric relations that are corporeal in nature rather than semantic. This is an important shift of perspective on several levels. For instance, it enables us to better appreciate the Heideggerean objection to the aesthetic attitude referred to earlier in which "art objects are implicitly understood as meaningful expressions of artists' lives that are capable of eliciting particularly intense or meaningful experiences in viewing subjects."[55] This focus on the corporeal, and intercorporeal, rather than the semantic—that is, on the communication or correspondence of forms—clearly also develops and diversifies the notion of the mimetic discussed earlier. But it does so in a particular way. According to Bersani, the communication of forms is a communication that "occurs either when the form of one thing speaks to the form of another, or when the elements of a single form speak among themselves."[56] Here again, phenomena of divestiture are inevitable. In Silverman's words, making reference to Bersani's 1995 book *Homos*: "Corporeal convergence is able to effect what the convergence of body and psyche cannot because, as Bersani puts it [...] the subject is at such moments 'so obscenely "rubbed" by the object it anticipates mastering that the very boundaries separating subject from object, boundaries necessary for possession [are] erased.'"[57] She continues:

> The dissolution of identity about which Bersani writes [...] is no more lasting than the erotic encounter through which it is effected. However,

when one body moves away from another, it leaves behind what might be called the "traces of difference." When the now solitary subject attempts to reconstitute itself, these traces of difference stick in the gears of the egoic machinery. The result is an inaccurate self-replication. In *Arts of Impoverishment* (1993), Bersani and Ulysse Dutoit dream of setting in motion an infinite series of these inaccurate self-replications. In *Homos,* Bersani intimates that inaccurate self-replication might also lead to an appetite for alterity, and so to a different relation to other creatures and things.[58]

And here, I cannot but recall the gritty textures that are pictured, for instance, in the opening sequence of Parker's film—those scenes of the abandoned pool with its covering of debris—and those which seem to permeate the pulsating, filmic surface of Nashashibi's *Stone and Table.* Indeed, returning to Parker's film, the perspectives offered by Silverman and Bersani prompt us to rethink the significance of what was earlier described as a possible ritualistic progression from a traumatized to an abundant—but non-subject-centered—scene. The key idea now being that each phase is vital and productive.

Which brings me, finally, to a third divestiture connected with intercorporeality, understood as the communication or correspondence of forms, namely the relinquishment of the idea that love, our most profound relational mode, is, above all, or exclusively, a feeling. This is a divestiture that by no means reduces love's extraordinary intimacy, but rather extends and intensifies it since, here, love is redefined as sets of actions or activities or practices, of patterns or forms of interaction that are marked by a particular kind of mimetic and compositional logic. Such a logic is hospitable to difference since it is not compelled to close the several uncomfortable gaps that are likely to become apparent within this process. It is a logic, furthermore, that does not inevitably place one or more human subjects at the center of things. Accordingly, this is an understanding of love that acknowledges alterity and, on a personal level, is also keen to gain a sense of productive distance on whatever happens to be our own current sense of self. Here relationship, love, and the ethical are indeed—and above all else—aesthetic matters. They are not, then, fundamentally a question of internalized feeling (although deep feelings are involved), nor of linguistics—of what is said, or promised, or proclaimed—but a question of the intercorporeal and compositional, out there, in the world. Earlier, I cited Bersani's description of intercorporeality as "a kind of spatial, anonymous narcissism." He has also defined the communication of forms in terms of "some other kind of sociality"[59] that is concerned, in the first instance, with "physical contacts, extensions, and correspondences," and with a shift from "a problematic of knowledge (and interiority) to a kind of cartography of the subject, a tracing of spatial connectedness."[60] In conversation with Bersani, Silverman responds affirmatively to this position, although her comments are again inflected in such a way as to focus on the human aspects of this relationality. She says:

> You remind us that the ego is in fact a form, although we don't usually think about it that way. [...] There is a lot to be gained through thinking about the ego in formal terms. First, it's deanthropomorphizing. It permits us to begin conceptualizing relationality outside of the usual human categories, which have become very reduced in recent years through the insistence upon race, class, gender, etc. It helps us to understand that what we are at the level of the ego may be a much more complex issue than we are accustomed to imagining, having to do not only with mothers, fathers, lovers, etc., but also with line, shape, composition, color.[61]

The outcome of this understanding is, in Bersani's words, "a solidarity not of identities but of positionings and configurations in space, one that even ignores the apparently most intractable identity difference: between the human and the non-human."[62] Crucially, though, this solidarity—like love, like every relationship that is not founded on mastery—is organized around a kind of inevitable openness, or brokenness. In response to this,

Bersani suggests that we must learn, from things, continually to refuse to fold back onto, or "into," ourselves. This, at least, is what seems to be indicated, each time in a differently inflected manner, not only in the work of these thinkers, but also in that category of non-effusive, understated, but formally and compositionally powerful, works of art of which Parker's and Nashashibi's films are instances. Works that I think unobtrusively but persistently participate in a broad project to elude the ongoing aspirations of the *subiectum* in its various contemporary guises: a project to redefine what could be meant by relationship, community, and sociality outside of the auspices of the exclusively human. Viewing work of this kind, there is a sense not of an invitation to enter (the non-communicative character of the work tends to preclude this), but, initially, simply to register or witness other relational trajectories. It is worth adding that, in the films by Parker and Nashashibi—as in the new genre of video painting referred to earlier—the camera, another nonhuman agent that has been set up deliberately in each case to operate as a non-expressive, static witness, seems to serve as an important existential model.

This essay started as a lecture, "Intending Objects and Signs 'Which Have No Meaning,'" presented at the Royal College of Art, London, January 2004. It has been revised and expanded for publication in this volume.

1 Jayne Parker, "Filmography," in *Jayne Parker: Filmworks 79–00* (Exeter: Spacex Gallery, 2000), 60.

2 "Foxfire Eins" was a solo exhibition of Parker's work held at the Spacex Gallery in Exeter in 2000 as part of a Film and Video Umbrella national tour. *Foxfire Eins* is also the title of a ten-minute, 16 mm black-and-white film made by Parker in 2000. It features cellist Anton Lukoszevieze's performance of Helmut Oehring's solo composition of the same name.

3 A. L. Rees, "The Artist as Filmmaker: Films by Jayne Parker, 1979–2000," in *Jayne Parker: Filmworks 79–00*, 12.

4 Ibid.

5 Johann Joachim Winckelmann, *Reflections on the Imitation of Greek Works in Painting and Sculpture* (La Salle, Illinois: Open Court, 1987), 33.

6 Jayne Parker in "The Frame—Jayne Parker" (2005), *Jayne Parker* (London: British Artists' Films, BFI, 2008), DVD.

7 Ibid.

8 Rees, "Artist as Filmmaker," 9.

9 Ibid.

10 Ibid.

11 Ibid., 18.

12 Ibid.

13 According to the website of Open Gallery, London, which is dedicated to video painting, this genre began with experiments carried out by the filmmaker and philosopher Hilary Lawson, and its rationale theorized by him in his book *Closure: A Story of Everything* (London: Routledge, 2001). See http://www.opengallery.co.uk/.

14 Barbara Bolt, *Heidegger Reframed* (London: I. B. Tauris & Co., 2011), 135.

15 Nicolas Bourriaud, *Relational Aesthetics*, trans. Simon Pleasance and Fronza Woods with Mathieu Copeland (Dijon: Les presses du réel, 2004), 8.

16 Ibid., 7.

17 Ibid., 16. "Over and above its mercantile nature and its semantic value, the work of art represents a social *interstice*. This *interstice* term was used by Karl Marx to describe trading communities that elude the capitalist economic context by being removed from the law of profit: barter, merchandising, autarkic types of production, etc. The interstice is a space in human relations which fits more or less harmoniously and openly into the overall system, but suggests other trading possibilities than those in effect within this system."

18 Ibid.

19 Ibid., 12.

20 Ibid., 12–13.

21 See Kaja Silverman, *World Spectators* (Stanford, CA: Stanford University Press, 2000).

22 Martin Heidegger, "The Age of the World Picture," in *The Question Concerning Technology and Other Essays*, trans. William Lovitt (New York: Harper and Row, 1977). The essay was first delivered in lecture form, and later published in 1950.

23 Iain D. Thomson, *Heidegger, Art, and Postmodernity* (Cambridge: Cambridge University Press, 2011), 40.

24 Heidegger, "Age of the World Picture," 128.

25 Ibid., 127.

26 Ibid., 134; brackets in original.

27 Ibid.

28 Ibid., 131, 134.

29 Ibid., 133.

30 Heidegger, "Age of the World Picture," 133.

31 Martin Heidegger, "The Origin of the Work of Art," trans. Alfred Hofstadter, in *Basic Writings: Martin Heidegger*, ed. David Farrell Krell (London: Routledge, 1978).

32 Thomson, *Heidegger, Art, and Postmodernity*, 43.

33 Heidegger, "Age of the World Picture," 116.

34 Thomson, *Heidegger, Art, and Postmodernity*, 50–51.

35 Heidegger, "Age of the World Picture," 134.

36 Ibid., 135–36.

37 Ibid., 136.

38 In book 2 of *On Painting*, Alberti refers to the "veil" (*velum*), which he also defined as "the intersection" (*intercisionem*), "whose usage I was the first to discover," a grid of threads stretched within a frame and set up as a guide between the painter and the objects to be painted. See Leon

Battista Alberti, *On Painting and On Sculpture*, trans. Cecil Grayson (London: Phaidon, 1972), 69. In order to enable proper proportioning in sculpture, Alberti refers in *On Sculpture* to an instrument called the *exempeda* and to the use of movable squares.

39 "Just as we see flat surfaces distinguished by their own lights and shades, so we may see spherical and concave surfaces divided up, as it were, in squares into several surfaces by different patches of light and shade" (ibid.).

40 Ibid., 87.

41 Ibid., 89; my emphasis.

42 Ibid., 63.

43 See, for example, Walter Benjamin's 1941 essay "A Small History of Photography," in *One-Way Street and Other Writings*, trans. Edmund Jephcott and Kingsley Shorter (London: Verso, 1985), 240–57.

44 Together with the art and film theorist Ulysse Dutoit, Bersani has written a number of important books including: *Arts of Impoverishment: Beckett, Rothko and Resnais* (Cambridge, MA: Harvard University Press, 1993); *Caravaggio's Secrets* (Cambridge, MA: MIT Press, 1998); and *Forms of Being: Cinema, Aesthetics, Subjectivity* (London: BFI Publishing, 2004).

45 Silverman, *World Spectators*, 129–30.

46 Tim Dean et al., "A Conversation with Leo Bersani," *October*, no. 82 (Autumn 1997): 4.

47 Silverman, *World Spectators*, 135.

48 Ibid., 143.

49 Ibid., 136.

50 Dean et al., "A Conversation with Leo Bersani," 14.

51 Ibid., 6.

52 Ibid.

53 See Roger Caillois, *The Writing of Stones*, trans. Barbara Bray (Charlottesville: University Press of Virginia, 1985), 95. This work was originally published as *L'écriture des pierres* in 1970.

54 Silverman, *World Spectators*, 139.

55 Thomson, *Heidegger, Art, and Postmodernity*, 50–51.

56 Silverman, *World Spectators*, 141.

57 Ibid., 142. Here, then, is also what Bersani calls an aesthetics of failure. Themes of attempted mastery and failure are also a repeated motif in several of Parker's films.

58 Ibid.

59 Dean et al., "A Conversation with Leo Bersani," 9.

60 Ibid., 8.

61 Ibid., 9.

62 Ibid., 14.

JA In recent years there's been a significant turn—in philosophy, in critical theory, and in art practice and theory—toward a new focus on objects, objecthood, and what has been called by some an object-orientated aesthetics. In my essay I talk about an object-generated aesthetics. As I see it, this isn't a regressive or nostalgic re-immersion in what some critics have called the autonomous, modernist logics of formalism, but something else. What do you think is going on, and why?

SO'S Yes, "object-orientated philosophy" is an offshoot, of a kind, from what has become known as "Speculative Realism," a philosophical movement of sorts that was "inaugurated" at a symposium of the same name here at Goldsmiths College, London, in 2007. There's lots to say about that, and especially, for myself, about identifying precursors to the Speculative Realist project in writers like Nick Land, and, more generally, Gilles Deleuze, Alain Badiou, and others. The latter two, in their own ways, allow for a move away from the "linguistic turn" of the humanities.

In the current context—and in relation to your essay—the concern with objects is part of a general interest in forms of thought that are not subsumed by subject–object determinations, or what Quentin Meillassoux has now famously dubbed a "correlationist" position (that is, that there can be no "knowledge" of the "Great Outdoors" that does not necessarily correlate with a given subject). Perhaps this is a reaction to those paradigms of textuality, discourse, and so forth, that have been hegemonic in the humanities in relatively recent times. Certainly, for myself, the writers associated with Speculative Realism have brought an inspiring and compelling voice to the humanities—

not least because they often communicate their ideas in a range of more para-academic sites and publications. I see something similar going on in your own essay, with its turn away from "relational aesthetics," away from human sociability as the horizon for thinking art, toward something more inhuman, if I can put it like that. In fact, your turn to Heidegger to think this terrain has resonances with Graham Harman's work, which also proceeds from a reading of that philosopher in laying out his object-orientated philosophy. It seems to me as if you have been paralleling this philosophical movement in your own work in visual culture. Harman's work lays out quite a complex idea of the object—and positions itself specifically against any philosophy that privileges the human–object relation above all others. I'm thinking that this is very similar to your own non-anthropocentric take on objects that attends to objects as agents, and to object–object relations—which in your case includes what we might call the object-like aspects of human beings too.

My recent interests are actually in the subject—or *subjectivity*—and, as such, might appear to be far from these concerns. But, in fact, the kind of subject I'm interested in is also a specifically nonhuman, or inhuman, one. I don't look at actor-network theory in order to delimit these nonhuman actors, but am interested, rather, in certain practices that might allow the subject-as-is—or *subiectum* as you call it in your essay—to become something other. Well, perhaps we can come back to this. To return to your essay, I want to ask you what specifically brought you to this interest in what you call object-generated aesthetics?

JA I would say it was three things. First, my experiences as a fine-art student in the 1980s; second, my experiences teaching art students in the 1990s; and third, seeing Cornelia Parker's 1998 show at the Serpentine Gallery in London. This was the show that had the actress

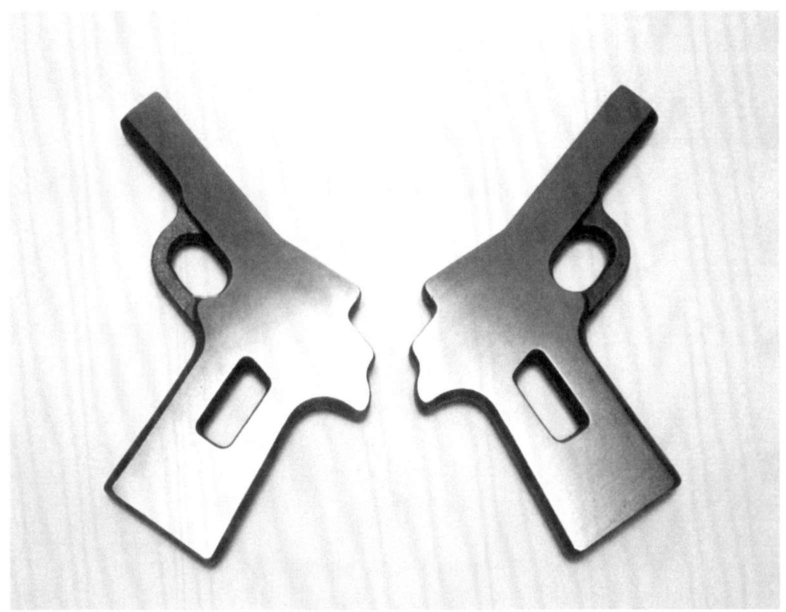

CORNELIA PARKER, *EMBRYO FIREARMS*, 1995. COLT .45 GUNS IN THE EARLIEST STAGE OF PRODUCTION, EDITION OF 2. COURTESY OF CORNELIA PARKER AND FRITH STREET GALLERY, LONDON.

Tilda Swinton sleeping in a glass display cabinet as its centerpiece. It also had a selection of often quite small or insignificant objects (like a feather from Freud's couch, or the swirls of black lacquer swarf that are left after a gramophone record has been cut) that all conveyed a strong sense of power, like religious relics. One piece in particular, *Embryo Firearms* (1995), had an extraordinary and lasting impact. These were two Colt .45 handguns that had been removed from the manufacturing process in the earliest stage of their production. They still had that slightly ambiguous shape that things have when they are coming into being (when they could still, potentially, be a number of possible things), but they'd been given the highly polished finish of a completed gun. They were positioned back to back, with their barrels turned outward, in such a way that the overall pattern they formed immediately made you think of those images used in Gestalt, and other forms of psychology, as diagnostic or projective tests. A Rorschach test, or even more appropriately in this case, the well-known "Rubin's vase" image, where the perceptual system keeps shifting between seeing either a centrally positioned vase, or two faces looking at each other, because it can't establish a stable figure–ground relationship.

Crucially, though, what struck me about *Embryo Firearms* was not that it made me think about my own perceptual or psychological make-up. On the contrary, the two objects or elements seemed to be setting off a kind of relational chain reaction—at the level of form and materiality—between themselves and the other objects in the room. I felt as though I was standing on the sidelines witnessing an extraordinary process taking place, one in which I was pretty much irrelevant. The thing is, this was a positive experience, exhilarating and enlarging. As I watched, I also had a sense of being presented with an expanded notion of the nature and location of thought. And it seemed important to hang on to the term "thought," even though it seemed to be occurring without human instigation or intervention. Later, I tried to think about it through what I called "material thought"—I taught a course with this title at Central Saint Martins when I was a visiting tutor there in 1997. In 2006, I tried to push these ideas further in an essay entitled "Critical Materialities," and now I'm trying again.

The essay in this book started out as a guest lecture I gave in 2004 to fine-art students—mainly students of painting, I think, at the Royal College of Art. The broader impetus was the plight of several students I was talking to while teaching, those who weren't going down the conceptual, or neo-conceptual approach to art making that was being pushed in a big way again in art schools in the 1990s—largely to counteract what many saw to be the regressive neo-expressionistic excesses of the 1980s. Against this cerebral tendency, students who were primarily drawn to the material processes of painting and of other forms of art making were struggling to justify their interests to themselves and others. They felt guilty, or at the very least concerned that they might be producing work that was culturally or politically irrelevant—or, worse, irresponsible.

My own training in the early 1980s was in painting and printmaking, and I'd struggled pretty unsuccessfully with those issues myself. It was only after I left college that I began to understand that the way I work best—the way I think best, if you like—is to let materials and processes have their way, without interfering or analyzing what's going on prematurely. While this means making ongoing leaps into the unknown that can be difficult to sustain, these leaps are not, in fact, into a void, but into very particular, specifically structured, material situations that become increasingly apparent. There is that incredible, addictive moment within the working process when things have flipped: the work itself has taken over and is directing its own construction; as an artist you just need to keep up. The same thing happens with writing. It's actually a common experience in everyday as well as creative life, but it can be hard to find the language to describe, let alone rationalize, it.

Having said all of that, though, I'd like to return the question. How did you get interested in this broad territory? Your essay "The Aesthetics of Affect" began as a lecture in 1999, didn't it? And then it was published a couple of years later in the journal *Angelaki*, which has as its remit the development of debates within the "theoretical humanities"?

SO'S Yes, my essay is certainly a symptom of its time—both my own history and in terms of what was happening in the humanities in the academy, at least in the UK. More on that—the context—in a moment, but first I just want to say that what you've just said about encountering an artwork, and how this makes demands, very much resonates with me. I've written elsewhere about a similar moment—for me—when I saw some work in Glasgow in the 1990s, and especially the abstract-figurative relation in Cathy Wilkes's work. To cut a long story short, I just didn't get Cathy's art when I first saw it: it stymied me and my interpretive strategies. But, of course, this was ultimately compelling, and it opened up a lot of trajectories in my thinking about what art is, what it does, and so on.

Anyway, to my essay. It was written at a time when deconstruction and ideology critique were hegemonic in the academy, at least within the discipline of art history—specifically with the "allegorical turn" of the *October* writers, the "New Art History," and the social history of art. My essay pitches itself against this field, hence the polemical tone and the "fall guys," especially Jacques Derrida and Theodor W. Adorno. In fact, this critical attitude came from my familiarity with these writers and this field, but also from feeling very hemmed in by it, caught in a kind of melancholy echo chamber—that was how I remember it. The essay was a way of trying to make a turn—an affective turn—away from all this, and especially away from the linguistic turn (and, as far as this goes, the essay resonates, at least to a certain extent, with the speculative turn I mentioned just now, which likewise announces a turn from the linguistic, textual, discursive). Gilles Deleuze and Félix Guattari, especially, were like a breath of fresh air for me. I first "encountered" them at the "Virtual Futures"conferences at Warwick University in the mid-1990s. And, as I indicated, the character of Nick Land was key. I subsequently taught an MA course at Leeds on "Materialist Aesthetics" where I developed the ideas—and did some reading—that later fed into my essay.

Anyway, this explains the tone of the essay, and the fact that, reading it now, the "enemies" are really caricatures or straw men—and the whole essay reads like a polemical ground-clearing exercise. In another way, even the thinkers I line myself up with are sometimes treated rather reductively. For example, given later translations, and the steady increase in secondary material, the conflation of Deleuze and Badiou—especially concerning the virtual—is very simplistic, and the implicit suggestion in my essay that Badiou's event might involve affects is, well, wrong. In fact, I also think that, although in the right direction, the Bergsonian-Spinozist idea of the virtual in the essay is a little confused (for what it's worth, I return to Henri Bergson, Baruch Spinoza, and to the Badiou-Deleuze contretemps in much more detail in my recently published monograph *On the Production of Subjectivity*).

All this said, I do think the general thrust of the essay, about attending to affect and asignification, about actualizing the virtual, of making visible the invisible—of art not being about representation, nor, indeed, about the crisis of representation—is an accurate record of my thoughts (and various points of inspiration) at the time. And it still needs to be said in today's expanded field of art practice and theory where, I think, there is still an abundance of "signifier enthusiasts," as I think Jean-François Lyotard once called them.

JA In fact, you went on to develop just this position, especially in relation to Deleuze and Guattari, in your first book, *Art Encounters Deleuze and Guattari.*

SO'S Yes, in fact, chapter two of that book was a longer version of the essay reprinted here. However, it is also worth noting that this "Deleuzian aesthetic" has, in many ways, become a new hegemony, and, as such, strange and contradictory strategies might be required—not least, perhaps, a turn back to the thinkers I pitched myself against in my essay. Certainly when I read your take on Adorno, it makes me want to go back and read him more carefully—from where I am now, as it were. In relation to all this, I do feel my essay contains quite a lot of Deleuzian jargon—but, again, this evidences a certain excitement, and even freedom, that Deleuze and Guattari's writings opened up for me at the time—specifically in thinking about art, but also, it has to be said, for my life more generally.

The last thing I want to say—concerning what, for me, is really a historical piece of writing—is that it was also written *for* the discipline of visual culture that was emerging at the time. Indeed, I first sketched out the polemic when I was leaving the University of Leeds, home of the more radical art histories mentioned above. I had completed my PhD there (on Adorno and Derrida, among others), and was moving to Goldsmiths—to what was then the "unit" of visual cultures in the department of Historical and Cultural Studies, but was soon to become its own department. Hence the appropriateness, nearly thirteen years later, of its appearing in one of the first volumes of our new "Visual Cultures as" series.

Anyway, to get back to our conversation, the focus of the essay is specifically on affect, a category of experience that, it seemed to me, had been evacuated from art history, or indeed art theory more generally (and I should say here that Brian Massumi's essay "The Autonomy of Affect," as my footnotes and the title of my own essay show, operated as an important model here). For you it's the category of "object," and the way it generates a certain kind of experience, that seems important. It occurs to me that this was also the terrain that Michael Fried's "Art and Objecthood" operated on, and, perhaps, a concern of modernism more generally. Fried's categories of absorption and theatricality seem to have resonances with some of what you write about objects. Would you agree?

JA Yes, but not in an altogether straightforward way. A value in art that is incredibly important for Fried is that it should display a kind of self-contained indifference to the beholder, a quality of "absorption." In the book *Absorption and Theatricality*, published in 1980 (in which he picks up on themes found in the seminal 1967 "Art and Objecthood" essay, and in which he develops the notion of absorption), he focuses on a constellation of French paintings from the second half of the eighteenth century in which "absorption" is very powerfully at play, like Chardin's now much-loved paintings of a boy building a house of cards, or his painting of a boy blowing soap bubbles. This phenomenon of absorption is one that I am drawn to and identify with.

Where Fried's oppositional understanding of the art–objecthood relationship is concerned, things get a bit more difficult. In the 1967 essay—and here, as Alex Potts has pointed out, his arguments were significantly shaped by local art politics—Fried claims that art is art only insofar as it defeats or suspends its own objecthood through what he calls "the medium of shape," that is, shape not as a fundamental property of objects but as a medium of painting. In other words, a beholder's engagement with art must occur at a nonliteral and purely optical level. He wrote this in counteraction to what he called the "literalist" (or Minimalist), and therefore "theatrical," art of Donald Judd, Robert Morris, and others—literal and theatrical because, according to Fried, these works lacked *internal* relationality (structurally and compositionally they asserted the values of wholeness, singleness, and indivisibility), which meant that they were necessarily directed toward, and required the presence of, viewers in order to have their effect.

As it turns out, I'm drawn to much of what Fried has to say about objecthood itself. But rather than see this as "antithetical to art," I'm really interested in precisely those works that Fried would define as nonart due to their aspiration "to discover and project objecthood as such." More broadly, I think it's interesting to consider why and how—in different periods or situations—artists have chosen to make work of this kind.

 So your engagement with "literalist" or Minimalist art has been rather different from the kinds of response that Fried describes?

 Yes. For me "literalist" art, with its emphasis on objecthood, not only has precisely those qualities of indifference, absorption, and presentness that Fried values, but also extends those qualities far beyond itself. I don't at all have the sense that art of this kind requires my presence in order to find completion. As with those pieces by Parker I referred to earlier, I find the works of Morris and Judd powerful for the specific ways in which they seem to open up sequences of nonhuman-centered relationships. In particular, they seem to me to emphasize the various physical, environmental, and intercorporeal structures of which they are a part, just at the level of being there—structures that I, as a viewer, am also embedded in; not in a central or controlling position, but more like another thing. I know that this will sound counterintuitive, but I think that this kind of awareness of our own nonhuman, and nonhuman-centered, modes of being is crucial for forging a profound sense of intimacy and connection with the world of other things, people, and situations. I think it is a kind of awareness we should aspire to.

Which brings me back, more directly, to questions about "affect." Early on in your essay you define affects as extra-discursive and extra-textual, and we've already talked about the affective turn, as you called it, as a turn away from what's arguably still an overly textualized approach to thinking and writing about art today. You then describe affects as "moments of intensity, a reaction in/on the body at the level of matter," and later you also refer to them in terms of sensations and forces. In everyday parlance, the term "affect" can also refer to emotion. So how does your position regarding the affective nature of art, and of our engagement with it, relate to long-standing and highly polarized debates about art and emotion? For instance, Wasily

Kandinsky famously wrote of his desire to fine tune—perhaps, in a sense, to systematize—art's capacity to impact the human soul and spirit, through the use of form, line, and color. And one of the earliest treatments of the relationship between art and emotion, to go back to basics, was the Aristotelian idea of catharsis as a critical function and effect of art. How does—or doesn't—your position relate to any of these?

SO'S I'm not sure about catharsis, but I'd say my own turn to affect was an attempt to return to a kind of intention, at least of sorts, in the face of the then-dominant paradigm of an expanded textuality that itself followed Barthes's "Death of the Author." I was interested, back then, in the idea of the artist, following Deleuze and Guattari, as the composer of blocs of affect. That said, you're correct in implying that the main thrust of my essay is in the idea of the effect an artwork has on its spectator/participant—specifically in producing affects. Affects, as I say in the essay itself, are not really about emotions, which, for me, come after, as a sort of secondary identification, or retroactive claiming of, affect (and, as such, are a very human technology); rather they name relations of intensity, increases and decreases in our sense of life—a specifically inorganic life (or even "life force," as I think you call it in your essay). As far as my position now goes, I'd say, following Spinoza, that affect and concept are really codeterminants; they are in a circle, if you like. So, really, concepts—or signifying regimes in general—are premised on certain combinations of affects. I've written a bit more about this in a relatively recent essay on Deleuze and contemporary art, but would say here that, for me, art is both asignifying (that is, operates through affect), but also signifying—inserting itself into a variety of signifying/discursive regimes. In fact, I'd say this is what makes art interesting: it is complex (again, different regimes of meaning) and simple (has an affective charge). So, art is a complex-simple object. For me, art that, for example, doesn't position itself as art, or make references to previous art, can be naive, and, in fact, a bit banal (and, not least, clichéd); but, on the other hand—as the Lyotard quote that begins my essay suggests—art that doesn't have an affective character as it were isn't really art. I guess what I'm claiming here, then, is that art *is* a kind of knowledge—or counter-knowledge, emergent knowledge—but also an event, a break in given regimes of knowledge.

I realize that you were asking about my relations of adjacency to debates in art history, but, as you can probably see, I don't really see my work as referencing these, at least not anymore. It's more the field of contemporary art production *and* continental philosophy that are my two areas of interest—the areas that I am most familiar with.

I said just now that I was interested in intention—that art has a specific direction, as it were, or intends something. Just to clarify, I don't think this intention comes from the artists really, it's more that the object, the artwork itself, has a kind of intention—often one that's hard to fathom in fact. Like a move in a game for which the rules are not entirely known. It's funny, but I'm drawn to this kind of complexity—or difficultness—it somehow forces me to think. I have the same reaction to "difficult" theoretical/philosophical work—its very density, almost its own object-like quality, attracts me. Your thesis on "material thought" seems to be implying something similar. Would you agree?

JA Yes, it's a central theme. But I'd want to make a distinction between intention, or indeed desire, and intentionality in the phenomenological sense (being intended or directed toward something)—and here, I'm interested in the ways in which objects, including artworks, display intentionality on a formal, material level. So there's a difference between what I'm trying to get at and, say, W. J. T. Mitchell's position in his influential essay "What Do Pictures Want?" Mitchell's essay, with some amendments, was republished in his 2005 book of the same name, but an early, shorter version appeared in 1996, in *October*, titled "What Do Pictures *Really* Want?" (The broader context here is Mitchell's longstanding focus on what he called the "pictorial turn." Like the "affective turn" we're interested in, it provides an alternative to semiotically oriented approaches to art.)

In "What Do Pictures Want?" Mitchell focuses on the issue of *desire* in relation to art, but instead of locating it either in the producers or consumers of images, he shifts "the location of desire to images themselves." He accepts the problems associated with this—the accusations he'd likely receive of anthropomorphizing, or subjectivizing objects, and so on—but as well as asking his readers to suspend disbelief, to get involved with what he calls a "thought experiment," he also argues that "the subjectivized, animated object in some form or other is an incurable symptom."[1] He says that "we are stuck with our magical, premodern attitudes toward objects, especially pictures, and our task is not to overcome these attitudes but to understand them, to work through their symptomatology."[2] If anything, I'm trying to move in the opposite direction, toward engagements—and an understanding also of humanness—in which notions of objecthood and intercorporeality are foregrounded.

Staying with Mitchell just a bit longer, it's probably also worth saying that by using the expression "What do pictures want?" he admits that he's purposefully, and again perhaps questionably, referencing tropes drawn from identity politics—Frantz Fanon's "What does the black man want?" or the question he attributes to Freud (which was also raised, with rather a different inflection, by feminism), "What do women want?"

SO'S The image as a kind of "subaltern"?

JA Yes. He explicitly associates his desiring entities (pictures) with the "abject or downcast Other" of identity politics—as you say, the "subaltern" who cannot speak for him- or herself but is spoken for by those in power. I can see why he is making this association, but I much prefer the way in which, at the end of the "What Do Pictures Want?" essay, he suddenly seems to move away from that subaltern definition of pictures to something more resistant. He writes, "What pictures want in the last instance, then, is simply to be asked what they want, with the understanding that the answer may well be nothing at all."[3]

SO'S I haven't much to say about Mitchell, beyond seeing, in what you've just said, elements of a common interest in a kind of nonhuman aesthetic. I'm certainly interested in this idea of a kind of desire immanent to pictures that is not "of" their producer. But in a way, the focus on pictures prevents me going further, as when I think of art—contemporary art—it's really the broader set of what has been called expanded art practices that I have in mind. Guattari has an interesting idea, which he borrows from Mikhail Bakhtin, about how art produces strange and different lines of desire. More specifically, he suggests that in the art experience, there is a "detachment of an ethico-aesthetic 'partial object' from the field of dominant significations" that "corresponds both to the promotion of a mutant desire and to the achievement of a certain disinterestedness."[4] I'm very taken with this, art as a kind of mutant center of subjectification, an autopoietic nucleus, or what Guattari calls a "Z or Zen point" around which a different kind of subjectivity might constellate or cohere. It seems to me that thinking about art in relation to the production of subjectivity offers something different than the more typical idea of a critical art practice that pitches itself against the ideological veils of the state or whatever. Well, there's lots more that could be said about this change in orientation—but, in the context of our conversation, I think this

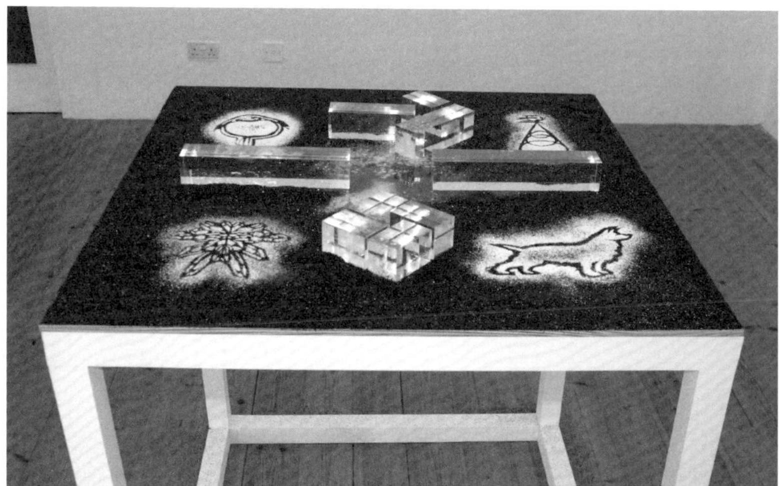

idea has strong resonances with what you say in your essay about the shadow, but even more specifically, following Roger Caillois, about the "enigmatic signifier" (and here, for example, I'm thinking Jacques Lacan's work might be worth revisiting for both of us). In a way this is a bit of a "secret" acephalic link between our two essays: Georges Bataille and Caillois, and a certain horizontality pitched against the verticality of the all-too-human.

JA What about the relation to actual art practice? A lot of what you've just said now seems to be particularly pertinent to practice.

SO'S Absolutely. In fact, the other key determining factor, at least in terms of my more recent ideas about art, is the practice I have, with David Burrows— Plastique Fantastique—that involves a kind of inquiry into the sacred *and* popular alongside (and through) various experiments in the production of subjectivity. Our collaboration involves objects, texts, installation, what we call shrines—but also performance. In many ways, these different kinds of production are about trying to find the alternative points of subjectification I mentioned just now. Performance, especially when it's a kind of absurdist stuttering and stammering, can open stuff up. It strikes me that this is something very similar to what you've already said about making art, how it begins to work on its own, or, in my terms, speaks back to its producer as if it came from an elsewhere. For me this is the reason to make art—to make, paradoxically, something that ultimately is not "of" you at all. Again, the essay of mine I mentioned about Deleuze and contemporary art develops some of these ideas. But in this specific context—and to return to some of the comments you made earlier—it's interesting that our theoretical, and academic, trajectories have been formed, at least in part, through practice. Almost as if we had to cross the line, access the other side, to really grasp what affects and objects—*material thought*—really is. In relation to this, one thing I found particularly striking about your essay—and that gives it another resonance with my own—is your interest in ritual, and the transformative potential of the latter. I was also struck by your interest in what, for me, is quite a Deleuzian theme: the inorganic life of things. Can I draw you out on these two themes?

JA Like you, the realm of the sacred is important to me. And although I wouldn't initially have said so, I suppose I am interested in ritual. In the context of these discussions, though—because we're trying to focus in on the asignifying registers of art, and of being more generally—I'm keen to put questions of content, or belief, or purpose, to one side. Instead, I want to focus on ritual as sets of ordinary, embodied actions that are repeated, temporally and spatially. Inevitably—*because* they are embodied and situated—they begin to structure both space and time perceptually and formally, creating environments, forging powerful connections with other entities, and so on. As we all know, by being repeated, these actions easily evade conscious awareness and conscious evaluation (they can also operate as blocks to awareness), and so can be both incredible productive and incredibly dangerous. That's why they're so important.

SO'S So, no belief, content, etcetera—but this does sound like an ethics...

JA Most debates about ethics focus on its rational or conscious aspects and on the nature of the principles, rules, commandments, laws that should be followed. And of course that's crucial. But the ethical isn't just a matter of conscious decision. There are embodied, intercorporeal dimensions to the ethical that have been expunged from the overly rationalized, modern mindset. What interests—and challenges—me is the idea that it's what we do habitually and unthinkingly (individually and collectively) that has the greatest force in terms of demonstrating who or what we are. The question is how to take this seriously too, and how to either advance or disrupt these behavioral levels of being, if and as necessary. We can underestimate—perhaps we prefer to underestimate—the impact of our ongoing, physical presence in the world. Not even what we do, but where and how we are positioned. But, without trying to get extreme, surely we've got to be accountable for that too.

So my interest is in what I'll call a layer of the ethical that has to do with our daily, habitual, and unreflected-upon functioning, the physical ways in which we inhabit space and time, the ways in which our gestures—including our facial gestures, smiles, or frowns—have an impact, on ourselves and others, of which we may rarely, or barely, be cognizant. For me, harking back to an earlier point in our conversation, this is where art as a resistant, asignifying, and profoundly influential force comes in—you also make this point in your essay. Encountering art at this level has a way of stopping us in our tracks, interrupting our usual ways of dealing with the world, and revealing alternate trajectories and connections at a physical and formal level. This also helps us register and reflect on those analogous, but often unreflected-upon, aspects of our own being, and, if need be, to introduce change. It's a vast and largely uncharted territory, and art practices—and modes of exhibition—that provide space for its exploration are vital.

This is also where I find the phenomenological work of Maurice Merleau-Ponty significant. Commentators often talk about the fact that he didn't devise an ethics as such, just as he didn't propose a politics as such. Nonetheless, his work has far-reaching ethical implications. And here, of particular interest to me is his writing about the body subject, and the habit body in the *Phenomenology of Perception*, and his later discussions of what he calls anonymous being: a layer of being that he felt Cézanne, in particular, picked up very profoundly in his paintings of things, places, and people. More broadly, of course, Merleau-Ponty's work is important in terms of challenging the legacy of Cartesian dualism. The lifelong challenge he'd set himself was how to think philosophically without recourse to models of thought that were (and still are) so overdetermined by subject–object relations— models in which subjects alone continue to have priority. Given all of this, and returning to our earlier discussions about the object-oriented character of recent philosophical thought—notably Speculative Realism—it's clear that the latter is one very interesting route into this territory, but that there are many other, older ones, including those that have their roots in art practice, and in phenomenology as a branch of philosophy that is particularly attuned and attentive to this world of lived experience and of lived practices.

SO'S So what about the issue of transformation?

JA In this context I'm probably thinking more about long, slow transformations. You usually can't track them step by step, but then you suddenly realize they've occurred. I'm emphasizing slowness because I wonder how often we mistake the inspiration to change, the revelation that change is possible, or its eventual manifestation (all of which can come in a flash), for actual change—of any kind, good or bad—which I think always takes time.

Finally—and this connects with that sense of long, slow change I was just talking about—I'm interested in an understanding of ritual and of transformation that is focused on accessing the here and now. In 1995–96, Siobhán Hapaska had a one-person show at the ICA in London called "Saint Christopher Legless." (The title alluded to the Catholic Church's decanonization of Saint Christopher, the patron saint of travelers—in 1968, I think—because he was no longer believed to have been a real person.) An especially powerful work in the exhibition was an organically shaped floor piece made from fiberglass. It looked like a kind of boat, certainly a vehicle of some kind, just large enough for one person to stretch out in. It was lined with a sheepskin, and came with straps, and an oxygen mask. You were invited to get into it, put on the straps and mask, and, one assumes, be transported somewhere: a metaphor, perhaps, for the idea that art is a vehicle of transportation (if not transformation). The title of the piece, however, was *Here* (1995). Hapaska said that the work was, in fact, designed to "do absolutely nothing because you shouldn't look at a piece of art and ask what will this piece of art do to me. [...] It's obviously not going to physically take you anywhere but I thought if I provided the right sensory conditions you might be able to think clearly. [...] This piece is not about escaping, physically or mentally."[5]

SO'S Ritual, for me, is about transformation—about certain practices that allow you to produce yourself differently. In my essay, I was thinking that perhaps all art might have this kind of ritualistic function (in addition to whatever else it might do). More recently, I've been thinking about this in relation to other "technologies of the self," as Michel Foucault called them. Not that this is to move away from art, but it is, rather, to expand art even further than "relational aesthetics": to think "life as a work of art," to use another phrase from Foucault.

Actually, for me, things are a little more complex than that. It seems to me that contemporary art practice is not really ritual in the proper sense, but, in fact, a kind of restaging of it. I don't mean it's ironic, but it is somehow knowing, self-reflexive. Perhaps an example would makes this more clear: In my life I have been involved in various ritual practices, but with Plastique Fantastique, although there is a sense that we do perform rituals, we are also well aware of the context—the spaces and places—of the practice, as well, of course, as the various art histories—performance, happenings, etcetera—that inform it. The practice has a certain *pitch* in this sense, as the art critic Robert Garnett once called it. In a way, then, I'd say that art practice exists in a kind of gray zone between ritual and the representation of it. Well, this is a bit of a tangent, but I wanted to say it, as it somehow relates to my more recent thinking around the signifying/asignifying aspects of art, and how these are both important.

JA And ethics?

SO'S Well, like you, all this means I'm interested in a kind of ethics—or perhaps that should be, following Guattari, an *ethico-aesthetics*. For myself, ethics is not really to do with good and bad, or the like—but, following Spinoza, is really an inquiry into what a body is capable of (insofar as we have no idea, really, what our body can do). This, for me, also has a certain political urgency. Capitalism tends to reduce the heterogeneity of life, to standardize it, especially in producing a homogenized "time" of the subject. In my latest book—sorry to keep returning to it, but it's foremost in my mind!—I'm interested in how we might excavate different times, alternative durations and temporalities, and foster new and different subjectivities to be produced (or, as I put it in the book, diagrams of the finite–infinite relation). In a way, this connects up with my essay in this book, insofar as such a subject—or, again *subjectivity*—is necessarily an intensive, affective one. I think this has a lot of resonance with what you've just said, and what you say in your essay, about a turn away from a certain, still prevalent Cartesian subject, and the regimes of knowledge, "understanding," and so forth, that are instantiated by the latter. In a way, it's a speculative subject that I'm interested in, a subject of Meillassoux's "Great Outdoors"— insofar as affect is this outdoors that is already in us, the outside folded in as Deleuze might have it. But this is also very much a pragmatic and processual project too—after all, it needs to be carried out in the present! Well, this, again, is more recent work. But the seeds of these ideas are there in my essay.

I mentioned capitalism just now—and I think it's crucial to link what can sometimes be quite rarefied and abstract research to our larger contemporary conditions. Of course, for both of us, these conditions include the state of Higher Education in the UK at the moment. Goldsmiths itself was at the forefront of some of the student occupations and teach-ins in 2011, and there were other art college teach-ins in London. How do you see your own work linking up with this political context, if at all?

JA I'm glad you've raised this question about the political and the pragmatic, because I was going to raise one final conundrum. In your text, you support a view of philosophy and art that is pragmatic, to do with practical problem solving. And in my essay I'm trying to be pragmatic and address a problem too: that of human-centeredness as an orientation that is, in fact, inimical to humanness in an ethical sense. I think there is something pragmatic about both of our views of visual culture. But this concern with pragmatics is very different, I think—I hope—to the pragmatics that are increasingly operative, in a top-down way, within education at all levels, and that is tied to a very reductive understanding about what it means to think, to work, to create, and so on. As we know, within political contexts in the UK and elsewhere, the arts and humanities are seen as valuable, and worth supporting, only if they can be guaranteed to quickly deliver identifiable outcomes, or if they are operating successfully in the context of the marketplace, making a profit, and providing well-paid jobs.

Where the political more broadly is concerned, all I can say is that here, as elsewhere, I'm always interested in detours and indirect routes. For me, this isn't a strategy of avoidance, but a way of opening up the affective character of a given context, as well as making space for more data (for that which may not be currently known), for getting repositioned, and so on. I think that if you address issues like the ones you're referring to without being willing to take those detours, you'll probably be addressing them in a reactive way, you'll be asking the wrong questions, and there probably won't be productive, longer-term outcomes. I think that art, in very specific, material ways, is very good at taking us down unanticipated but often, ultimately, productive detours of this kind.

SO'S I'd certainly agree with that. Art isn't politics; it operates through its own protocols and logics. For myself, it is especially the way it breaks with existing regimes of knowledge—or information, really— and offers alternative narratives. A scrambling of the codes and the production of autonomous ones, as Deleuze and Guattari might have it. As far as this goes, then, perhaps pragmatics isn't exactly the right word. Art, for me, involves a kind of super-productivity, but one that is pitched against the typical emphasis on productivity in the work- and marketplace. In terms of what's happening with the academy, at present, I'd say these artistic strategies—as I suggested before—take on a political urgency, in the sense that, put simply, they are the imagining of alternatives.

More recently, I've been thinking about art practice as the construction of different collective imaginings—the production of a kind of counter-unconscious to the one currently being promised by and produced through commodity culture. Ultimately, I think, this links to some of the material in my essay, as it seems to me that it's precisely on the terrain of affect—of affective modulation—that the battle against the homogenizing and paralyzing powers of capitalism must take place: in Spinoza's terms, the crucial question concerns what increases your capacity to act, to simply exist, in the world—and what does the opposite.

1   W. J. T. Mitchell, "What Do Pictures Want?,"
    in *What Do Pictures Want? The Lives and Loves
    of Images* (Chicago: University of Chicago Press,
    2005), 30.
2   Ibid.
3   Ibid., 48.
4   Félix Guattari, *Chaosmosis: An Ethico-Aesthetic
    Paradigm*, trans. Julian Pefanis and Paul Bains
    (Sydney: Power Institute of Fine Arts, 1995), 13.
5   "Siobhán Hapaska in Conversation with Ingrid
    Swenson: January 1996," in *Siobhán Hapaska*
    (London: Institute of Contemporary Arts, 1996),
    n.p.

BIBLIOGRAPHY

Adorno, Theodor W. *Aesthetic Theory.* Translated by Christian Lenhardt. London: Routledge, 1984.

———. *Minima Moralia: Reflections on a Damaged Life.* Translated by E. F. N. Jephcott. London: Verso, 1978.

Alberti, Leon Battista. *On Painting and On Sculpture.* Translated by Cecil Grayson. London: Phaidon, 1972.

Andrews, Jorella. "Critical Materialities." In *A.C.A.D.E.M.Y.* Edited by Angelika Nollert et al., 178–86. Frankfurt am Main: Revolver Verlag, 2006.

Badiou, Alain. *Deleuze: The Clamor of Being.* Translated by Louise Burchill. Minneapolis: University of Minnesota Press, 1999.

Bann, Stephen. "Three Images for Kristeva: From Bellini to Proust." *Parallax* 4, no. 3 (1998): 65–79.

Bataille, Georges. *Prehistoric Painting: Lascaux or the Birth of Art.* Translated by Austryn Wainhouse. London: Macmillan, 1980.

Benjamin, Andrew. *The Plural Event: Descartes, Hegel, Heidegger.* London: Routledge, 1993.

Benjamin, Walter. "A Small History of Photography." In *One-Way Street and Other Writings.* Translated by Edmund Jephcott and Kingsley Shorter, 240–57. London: Verso, 1985.

Bergson, Henri. *Matter and Memory.* Translated by Nancy Margaret Paul and W. Scott Palmer. New York: Zone Books, 1991.

Bersani, Leo and Ulysse Dutoit. *Arts of Impoverishment: Beckett, Rothko and Resnais.* Cambridge, MA: Harvard University Press, 1993.

———. *Forms of Being: Cinema, Aesthetics, Subjectivity.* Cambridge, MA: MIT Press, 2004.

———. *Caravaggio's Secrets.* Cambridge, MA: MIT Press, 1998.

Bogue, Ronald. "Art and Territory." In *A Deleuzian Century?* Edited by Ian Buchanan, 265–69. Durham, NC: Duke University Press, 1999.

———. "Gilles Deleuze: The Aesthetics of Force." In *Deleuze: A Critical Reader.* Edited by Paul Patton, 257–69. Oxford: Blackwell, 1989.

Bolt, Barbara. *Heidegger Reframed.* London: I. B. Tauris & Co., 2011.

Bourriaud, Nicolas. *Relational Aesthetics.* Translated by Simon Pleasance and Fronza Woods with Mathieu Copeland. Dijon: Les presses du réel, 2004.

Burgin, Victor. *The End of Art Theory: Criticism and Postmodernity.* London: Macmillan, 1986.

Caillois, Roger. *The Writing of Stones.* Translated by Barbara Bray. Charlottesville: University Press of Virginia, 1985.

Dean, Tim et al. "A Conversation with Leo Bersani." *October*, no. 82 (Autumn 1997): 3–16.

Deleuze, Gilles. *Bergsonism.* Translated by Hugh Tomlinson and Barbara Habberjam. New York: Zone Books, 1991.

———. *Difference and Repetition.* Translated by Paul Patton. London: Athlone Press, 1994.

———. *Negotiations: 1972–1990.* Translated by Martin Joughin. New York: Columbia University Press, 1995.

———. "Spinoza and the Three Ethics." In *Essays Critical and Clinical.* Translated by Dan W. Smith and Michael A. Greco, 139–51. London: Verso, 1998.

Deleuze, Gilles and Félix Guattari. *A Thousand Plateaus: Capitalism and Schizophrenia.* Translated by Brian Massumi. London: Athlone, 1994.

———. *What Is Philosophy?* Translated by Graham Burchill and Hugh Tomlinson. London: Verso, 1994.

de Man, Paul. "Literary History and Literary Modernity." In *Blindness and Insight: Essays in the Rhetoric of Contemporary Criticism*, 142–65. London: Routledge, 1989.

Derrida, Jacques. "The Parergon." In *The Truth in Painting.* Translated by Geoff Bennington and Ian McCleod, 37–82. Chicago: University of Chicago Press, 1987.

Forster, Kurt W. "Critical History of Art, or a Transfiguration of Values?" *New Literary History* 3, no. 3 (Spring 1972): 459–70.

Guattari, Félix. *Chaosmosis: An Ethico-Aesthetic Paradigm*. Translated by Julian Pefanis and Paul Bains. Sydney: Power Institute of Fine Arts, 1995.

———. "On Machines." Translated by Vivian Constantinopoulos. In *Complexity: Architecture/Art/ Philosophy*. Edited by Andrew E. Benjamin, 8–12. London: Academy, 1989.

Hapaska, Siobhán. "Siobhán Hapaska in Conversation with Ingrid Swenson: January 1996." In *Siobhán Hapaska*. London: Institute of Contemporary Arts, 1996.

Heidegger, Martin. "The Age of the World Picture." In *The Question Concerning Technology and Other Essays*, 116–36. Translated by William Lovitt. New York: Harper and Row, 1977.

——— "The Origin of the Work of Art." Translated by Alfred Hofstadter. In *Basic Writings: Martin Heidegger*. Edited by David Farrell Krell, 149–87. London: Routledge, 1978.

Lawson, Hilary. *Closure: A Story of Everything*. London: Routledge, 2001.

Lyotard, Jean-François. *Peregrinations: Law, Form, Event*. New York: Columbia University Press, 1988.

———. "Philosophy and Painting in the Age of Their Experimentation: Contribution to an Idea of Postmodernity." Translated by M. Minich Brewer and Daniel Brewer. In *The Lyotard Reader*. Edited by Andrew Benjamin, 181–95. Oxford: Blackwell, 1989.

———. *The Postmodern Condition: A Report on Knowledge*. Translated by Geoff Bennington and Brian Massumi. Manchester: Manchester University Press, 1984.

———. "The Tensor." Translated by Seán Hand. In *The Lyotard Reader*. Edited by Andrew Benjamin, 1–18. Oxford: Blackwell, 1989.

Massumi, Brian. "The Autonomy of Affect." In *Deleuze: A Critical Reader*. Edited by Paul Patton, 217–36. Oxford: Blackwell, 1989.

Melville, Stephen. "Notes on the Reemergence of Allegory, the Forgetting of Modernism, the Necessity of Rhetoric, and the Conditions of Publicity in Art and Art Criticism." *October*, no. 19 (1981): 55–92.

Mitchell, W. J. T. "What Do Pictures Want?" In *What Do Pictures Want? The Lives and Loves of Images*, 30–48. Chicago: University of Chicago Press, 2005.

O'Sullivan, Simon. "The Aesthetics of Affect: Thinking Art beyond Representation." *Angelaki* 6, no. 3 (2001): 125–35.

———. *Art Encounters Deleuze and Guattari: Thought beyond Representation*. Basingstoke: Palgrave, 2005.

———. "From Aesthetics to the Abstract Machine: Deleuze, Guattari, and Contemporary Art Practice." In *Deleuze and Contemporary Art*. Edited by Stephen Zepke and Simon O'Sullivan, 189–207. Edinburgh: Edinburgh University Press, 2010.

———. "In Violence: Three Case Studies against the Stratum." *Parallax* 6, no. 2 (2000): 115–21.

———. *On the Production of Subjectivity: Five Diagrams of the Finite–Infinite Relation*. Basingstoke: Palgrave, 2012.

———. "Writing on Art (Case Study: The Buddhist Puja)." *Parallax* 7, no. 4 (2001): 115–21.

Owens, Craig. "The Allegorical Impulse: Towards a Theory of Postmodernism." *October*, no. 12 (1980): 67–86.

Parker, Jayne. "Filmography." In *Jayne Parker: Filmworks 79–00*. Exeter: Spacex Gallery, 2000.

———. "Foxfire Eins." Solo exhibition at the Spacex Gallery, Exeter, 2000.

———. "The Frame—Jayne Parker." *Jayne Parker*. DVD, 2005. London: British Artists' Films, BFI, 2008.

Potts, Alex. *The Sculptural Imagination: Figurative, Modernist, Minimalist*. New Haven, CT: Yale University Press, 2000.

Rajchman, John. "Abstraction." In *Constructions*, 55–75. Cambridge, MA: MIT Press, 1998.

Rees, A. L. "The Artist as Filmmaker: Films by Jayne Parker, 1979–2000." In *Jayne Parker: Filmworks 79–00*, 9–18. Exeter: Spacex Gallery, 2000.

Silverman, Kaja. *World Spectators*. Stanford, CA: Stanford University Press, 2000.

Stivale, Charles J. "Pragmatic/Machinic: Discussion with Félix Guattari." March 19, 1985. http://topologicalmedialab.net/xinwei/classes/readings/Guattari/Pragmatic-Machinic_chat.html.

Thomson, Iain D. *Heidegger, Art, and Postmodernity*. Cambridge: Cambridge University Press, 2011.

Winckelmann, Johann Joachim. *Reflections on the Imitation of Greek Works in Painting and Sculpture*. La Salle, IL: Open Court, 1987.

BIOGRAPHIES

Jorella Andrews's research focuses on the relations between art practice, perception, and philosophical inquiry, with an emphasis on phenomenology. She is the "Visual Cultures as..." series editor.

Simon O'Sullivan works between art practice, philosophy, and modern and contemporary art theory. His particular interests are in aesthetics, ritual and performance, psycho/schizoanalysis, and the production of subjectivity. He is also part of the "performance fiction" Plastique Fantastique with David Burrows.

Jorella Andrews and Simon O'Sullivan
VISUAL CULTURES AS **OBJECTS AND AFFECTS**

Published by Goldsmiths, University of London
and Sternberg Press

Series editor: Jorella Andrews
Series assistant editor: Jon K. Shaw
Editor: Leah Whitman-Salkin
Proofreader: Max Bach
Design: Marit Münzberg
Printing and binding: Lecturis, Eindhoven

Cover image: Plastique Fantastique, *Protocols for Deceleration: Night is also a Sun*, Outpost Gallery, Norwich, UK, November 2009 (detail)
Photo: Silke Blohm

ISBN 978-3-943365-38-2

Goldsmiths, University of London
New Cross
London SE14 6NW
UK
www.gold.ac.uk

Sternberg Press
Caroline Schneider
Karl-Marx-Allee 78
D-10243 Berlin
www.sternberg-press.com

Other titles in this series include
VISUAL CULTURES AS **RECOLLECTION**
VISUAL CULTURES AS **SERIOUSNESS**